Learning F# Functional Data Structures and Algorithms

Get started with F# and explore functional programming paradigm with data structures and algorithms

Adnan Masood, Ph.D.

[PACKT] open source*
PUBLISHING   community experience distilled

BIRMINGHAM - MUMBAI

Learning F# Functional Data Structures and Algorithms

First published: June 2015

Production reference: 1240615

Published by Packt Publishing Ltd.
Livery Place
35 Livery Street
Birmingham B3 2PB, UK.

ISBN 978-1-78355-847-6

www.packtpub.com

Credits

Author
Adnan Masood, Ph.D.

Reviewers
Steve Bearman

Taha Hachana

Marcin Juraszek

Rohit Pathak

Commissioning Editor
Kunal Parikh

Acquisition Editor
Shaon Basu

Content Development Editor
Rahul Nair

Technical Editor
Parag Topre

Copy Editors
Relin Hedly

Sonia Mathur

Project Coordinator
Nidhi Joshi

Proofreaders
Stephen Copestake

Safis Editing

Indexer
Monica Ajmera Mehta

Graphics
Disha Haria

Jason Monteiro

Production Coordinator
Nilesh R. Mohite

Cover Work
Nilesh R. Mohite

Foreword

Functional programming is about to become mainstream, and learning F# helps a programmer build skills in multiple paradigms. It doesn't surprise me at all that Adnan has found his way to functional programming. His dedication to technological excellence is expressed eloquently in this book, and if you want to get started with F#, this is the book to read.

Jon Flanders

Pluralsight Trainer, Microsoft MVP

Foreword

In the era of multiprocessor and multimachine processing, functional principles are becoming increasingly important for modern programmers. For those developing in the Microsoft ecosystem, F# is a functional first multiparadigm language that allows practitioners to apply these principles in a truly powerful way. As developers become more familiar with functional data structures and the algorithms that use them truly safely, by extension, powerful software will become a more commonplace commodity that will drive the next era of technological innovation. I can't think of a more thorough and thoughtful person to help guide us through these principles than Adnan. Enjoy!

Seth Juarez

Senior Technical Evangelist, Microsoft

Foreword

F# is a functional and object-oriented programming language with the power of the .NET Framework. This language has gained huge popularity among a broad range of programmers. With a focus on writing simple code to solve complex problems, F# is being used by data scientists, enterprise developers, and enterprise enthusiasts. In fact, its popularity has increased so much in recent times that according to the TIOBE index (ranked 11th as of March 2015), F# is all set to gain an esteemed position among the top 10 programming languages.

With the rise in interest and usage around F#, it's bound to continue to attract the attention of hobbyists who want to try out writing programs with F#. I am very excited about Adnan Masood's efforts and appreciative of his work, which focuses on the basics of functional programming, data structures, and algorithms. Adnan has followed a very structured approach to take you on a journey where you can discover and familiarize yourself with this powerful multiparadigm programming language. Starting with setting the context and discussing the basics of F# programming, Adnan gradually moves on to a more detailed and increasingly focused conversation surrounding data structures and algorithms. He also covers approaches related to testing bespoke data structures and algorithms. Towards the end, Adnan covers the implementation of modern and complex abstract data types (ADTs) and highlights how to use parallel programming and asynchrony within the F# setting.

I highly recommend this book and ask you to focus your energies on learning this amazing and powerful multiparadigm, open source, and cross-platform programming language. This book will help you tackle computing problems with a simple, maintainable, and robust code.

Happy F# Programming.

Hammad Rajjoub

Architect Advisor, Mobility Lead (Asia), Microsoft

About the Author

Adnan Masood, Ph.D. is a developer, software architect, and researcher and specializes in machine learning and Bayesian belief networks. He is an avid engineer and is most comfortable working with the IDE. Before joining Green Dot Corporation, a leading prepaid financial technology institution, he enjoyed life as a principal engineer of a start-up and worked for a leading UK nonprofit organization as a solutions architect.

A strong believer in the development community, Adnan is an active member of the Open Web Application Security Project (OWASP), an organization dedicated to software security. In the .NET community, he is a cofounder and president of the Pasadena .NET Developers group, which he has been successfully leading for 8 years. He pursues interests in algorithmic puzzles, machine learning, functional programming, cloud computing, service-oriented architecture (SOA), .NET, design patterns, application security, and robotics. He has also led a number of successful enterprise solutions and consulted for several Fortune 500 company projects.

Adnan devotes himself to his own continual, practical education. He holds certifications in big data, machine learning, and systems architecture from Massachusetts Institute of Technology; an Application Security certification from Stanford University; an SOA Smarts certification from Carnegie Mellon University; and certifications as a ScrumMaster, Microsoft Certified Trainer, Microsoft Certified Solutions Developer, and Sun Certified Java Developer.

Adnan has taught Windows Communication Foundation (WCF) courses at the University of California, San Diego, and loves to conduct presentations at top academic and technology conferences (for example, IEEE-HST, IASA, and DevConnections), local code camps, and user groups. He is also a volunteer FLL robotics coach for middle school students at Universal Academy of Florida.

At home, his two very energetic boys, Zakariya and Ali, keep him busy — but not quite busy enough to keep him from compulsively buying (though not always reading) books in all formats. Adnan defines Pluto as a planet, chocolate as a food group, and *A Game of Thrones* as historical fiction.

For more details, visit Adnan's blog (`http://blog.adnanmasood.com`), GitHub repository (`http://github.com/adnanmasood`), and Twitter (`@adnanmasood`). Adnan can be reached at `adnan.masood@owasp.org`.

Acknowledgments

I am very grateful to the technical reviewers—Steve Bearman, Taha Hachana, Marcin Juraszek, and Rohit Pathak—whose meticulous reviews proved invaluable in improving the quality of this book. Thank you for your diligence and your help throughout the process. Thanks to the excellent team at Packt Publishing. I would also like to thank the technical editor, Parag Topre, and the content development editor, Rahul Nair, who worked with me and kept this project on track to publish this book. Your assistance as an editor and reviewer along with your comments were invaluable in ensuring that this book was a comprehensive and reliable source of information on F# and functional programming.

Thanks to Don Syme and Microsoft Research, without whom neither F# nor this book would have been possible, and to the excellent F# community that provides plenty of resources. It has been my privilege to work closely with Jeff Bergman (Google), who got me started on F# and functional programming. I am forever grateful to Stephen Soong, for his unwavering support and feedback, and David Lazar, who allowed me to run seemingly crazy ideas by him. I am indebted to all my friends and colleagues, including Nicolas Naaman, David Gullett, Calvin Park, Teresa Watkins, Raja Peer, Dave Banta, Ajit Kumar, Dr. Jevdet Rexhepi, Paul Watson, Dr. John Dean, Kamran Masood, Jim Java, Muhammad Mansoor, Antony Chhan, Rashid Kamran, Jeff Cox, Mobeen Minai, Rob Walling, and Kamran Zameer, to name a few, for reading the early drafts and providing feedback and encouragement. And last but not least, special thanks to my family for their support and to my kids, Zakariya and Ali; without their shenanigans, this book would have been finished 6 months earlier. Love you guys!

About the Reviewers

Steve Bearman is a software developer with his own software and consulting company, Suzy B Studios. He supports all sectors from science and engineering through business and finance and specializes in the thorny, complex problems where architecture, algorithms, performance, and usability are critical. He has been developing with .NET for over a decade. He has long been functionally oriented; one of his first preferred programming languages, years ago, was the early functional, mathematical programming language APL.

Steve has a special fondness for good algorithms and appropriate technology. He has taught university graduate-level computer science and managed marketing and operations as the VP of a manufacturing corporation. Steve has published technical papers dealing with data, its analysis, interpretation, and automated collection. He speaks frequently on technical topics. He has an SB in Mathematics from MIT and an MA in applied mathematics, concentrating on algorithms and mathematical statistics, from the University of California, San Diego.

He enjoys life with his beautiful wife and two dogs, holds black belts in two styles of martial arts, juggles, rides his unicycle, and enjoys the arts and the outdoors.

Taha Hachana is an enthusiast F# hacker. He has been using this language since 2008 (2 years before it became a Microsoft product). As an active community member, he has been maintaining several open source F# projects on GitHub, focusing on web development with the WebSharper framework and data visualization. When he's not coding, Taha enjoys practicing martial arts and yoga. You can follow him on Twitter at @TahaHachana and read his blog at http://fsharp-code.blogspot.com/.

Marcin Juraszek is a software engineer at Microsoft. He is associated with Office Online, a web browser-based version of the Microsoft Office productivity suite.

He holds bachelor's of engineering and master's of science degrees in computer science from the Silesian University of Technology in Gliwice, Poland. Before moving to the U.S., Marcin worked at Future Processing, one of the fastest growing software companies in central and eastern Europe.

He has been a .NET developer since the last 4 years. His expertise spans across most of .NET stack, including C#, VB.NET, F#, ASP.NET, XAML, WPF, Silverlight, LINQ, and .NET Core. He's also interested in new technologies, such as TypeScript, Azure, Roslyn, and so on.

He runs his own programming-oriented blog at `http://marcinjuraszek.com` and is an active member of the Stack Overflow community.

Rohit Pathak has a degree in computer science from Rajiv Gandhi Technical University. He picked up his interest in functional programming while working on High Performance Computing (HPC) at AITR (Acropolis Institute of Technology and Research). For years, he worked at Innovation at Incubation Labs and NTI (NEC Technologies India Limited), focusing on machine learning, static model checking, compilers, and HPC. Currently, he is working as a lead software engineer with the system and verification group at Cadence Design Systems.

www.PacktPub.com

Support files, eBooks, discount offers, and more

For support files and downloads related to your book, please visit www.PacktPub.com.

Did you know that Packt offers eBook versions of every book published, with PDF and ePub files available? You can upgrade to the eBook version at www.PacktPub.com and as a print book customer, you are entitled to a discount on the eBook copy. Get in touch with us at service@packtpub.com for more details.

At www.PacktPub.com, you can also read a collection of free technical articles, sign up for a range of free newsletters and receive exclusive discounts and offers on Packt books and eBooks.

https://www2.packtpub.com/books/subscription/packtlib

Do you need instant solutions to your IT questions? PacktLib is Packt's online digital book library. Here, you can search, access, and read Packt's entire library of books.

Why subscribe?

- Fully searchable across every book published by Packt
- Copy and paste, print, and bookmark content
- On demand and accessible via a web browser

Free access for Packt account holders

If you have an account with Packt at www.PacktPub.com, you can use this to access PacktLib today and view 9 entirely free books. Simply use your login credentials for immediate access.

Table of Contents

Preface

"If there's a book that you want to read, but it hasn't been written yet, then you must write it."

– *Toni Morrison*

F# is a multiparadigm programming language that encompasses object-oriented, imperative, and functional programming language properties. The functional paradigm can be defined as programming with pure functions, programming by function composition, and a combination of both. For over a quarter of a century, functional programming languages such as Lisp, Haskell, and standard ML existed in academia, but industry adaption has been quite slow. With the introduction of F#, an open source functional programming language, this trend is witnessing a significant change. F# runs on the .NET runtime and supports libraries from other IL-based programming languages.

Due to the seemingly overarching title of this manuscript, a few disclaimers are in order. This book is an introduction to F#, functional data structures, and algorithms. These topics are fairly large in their individual capacity. A large body of growing literature exists in each of these areas itself. Therefore, it won't be a reasonable expectation to provide a comprehensive picture of data structures and algorithms in the limited amount of space available in this book. Instead, this book is intended as a cursory introduction to the use and development of data structures and algorithms using F#. The goal is to provide a broader overview and resources to the reader to get started with functional programming using F#.

This book is written with a few assumptions, keeping the reader in mind. We assume that the reader has basic knowledge of an imperative programming language and object-oriented concepts. Readers are highly encouraged to try out examples, use the resources listed in *Chapter 10, Where to Go Next?*, and review specialized texts for a more comprehensive treatment of algorithms and data structures.

Starting with the basic concepts of F#, this book will help you to solve complex computing problems with simple, maintainable, and robust code. Using easy-to-understand examples, you will learn how to design data structures and algorithms in F# and apply these concepts in real-life projects, as well as gain insights into how to reuse libraries available in community projects. You will also learn how to set up Visual Studio .NET and F# compiler to work together, implement the Fibonacci sequence and Tower of Hanoi using recursion, and apply lazy evaluation for quick sorts. The book will then cover built-in data structures and take you through enumerations and sequences. You will gain knowledge about stacks, graph-related algorithms, and implementations of binary trees. Next, you will understand the custom functional implementation of a queue and look at the already available collection and concurrent collection structures. You will also review sets and maps and explore the implementation of a vector.

In the final leg of this book, you will find resources and references that will give you a great overview of how to build an application in F# and do great things. We have tried our best to provide attribution to all the resources used in this book. However, if anything has been missed, let us know. To build upon the fundamentals you would learn in this book, we have created a code repository to solve project Euler algorithmic problems. Project Euler is a series of challenging mathematical and computer programming problems that require working with algorithms and data structures. You will see our solutions on the GitHub repo at `https://github.com/adnanmasood/Euler.Polyglot`.

In the cover, the choice of lush landscape and central figure reminiscent of general Sherman trail is an attempt to portray the variety of programming paradigms and the potential strength of functional concepts. In the words of Ryan Bozis, learn these functional constructs, and you'll be able to program your very own forest. Being polyglot is good! Learning a new programming language broadens your thinking and provides you a competitive edge. Happy functional programming!

What this book covers

Chapter 1, Embrace the Truth, explains F#'s rather special role in the functional programming world. You will also discuss F#'s roots in ML, the context in which F# works, that is, running on top of .NET stack, compiled to IL, utilizing BCL and the hybrid nature of the languages.

Chapter 2, Now Lazily Get Over It, Again, will prepare you to delve into the intermediate F# concepts which you are going to utilize later. It will help you in setting up the Visual Studio .NET and F# Compiler to work together along with the environment and runtime, review how to run your F# programs in IDE and through interactive REPL shell, implement the Fibonacci sequence and Tower of Hanoi using recursion, and apply lazy evaluation for quick sort.

Chapter 3, What's in the Bag Anyway?, will provide insights about the built-in data structures—array, list, set, and map, and will present their typical use cases.

Chapter 4, Are We There Yet?, delves into sequence expression (seq), implementation of custom enumeration for purpose of sequence expression (that is, paging functionality), and application of simple custom types using records, tuples.

Chapter 5, Let's Stack Up, will help you build a basic ADT of a stack using F#, implement the fundamental operations, and proceed to make a concurrent version of a stack. You will also learn how to do unit testing in C# for an F# program and implement the same test method in F#.

Chapter 6, See the Forest for the Trees, will explain graph related algorithms, and teach you the implementation of your own trees. You will also learn to tackle tree searching and various other traversal techniques.

Chapter 7, Jumping the Queue, discusses the custom functional implementation of a queue. You will then be introduced to the FSharpX open source collection of functional data structures. Finally, you will explore the F# agent of MailboxProcessor, for creating async work flows, throttling, and post-processing of the results of asynchronous calls as an example usage of a queue.

Chapter 8, Quick Boost with Graph, will briefly discuss how a graph can be implemented in a functional language, and why it is a rather difficult task to undertake. You will then discover some commonly used graph implementations and explore one of the most typical shortest path graph implementation, Dijkstra.

Chapter 9, Sets, Maps, and Vectors of Indirections, reviews sets and maps, and explores a custom implementation of a vector. Additionally, you are going to discuss Intermediate Language and how it works in the .NET ecosystem.

Chapter 10, Where to Go Next?, is a reference chapter in which you can acquaint yourself with the detailed list of different resources around the functional eco-system, and the F# programming language. You will also find various guides, source code and links, which will assist you in getting additional information you will need to polish your knowledge about F#.

What you need for this book

To get started with working on F#, you will need Visual Studio 2013. Also, you will need Windows or Linux/MacOS with Mono to build the server, console and GUI applications. Visual Studio 2013 Professional/Community Edition is preferred.

Who this book is for

If you have just started your adventure with F#, then this book will help you take the right steps to become a successful F# programmer, thereby improving your current development skills. Intermediate knowledge of imperative programming concepts and a basic understanding of the algorithms and data structures in .NET environments using the C# language and BCL (Base Class Library) would be helpful.

Conventions

In this book, you will find a number of text styles that distinguish between different kinds of information. Here are some examples of these styles and an explanation of their meaning.

Code words in text, database table names, folder names, filenames, file extensions, pathnames, dummy URLs, user input, and Twitter handles are shown as follows: " You can also use the `#help;;` directive to list other directives inside FSI."

A block of code is set as follows:

```
val cubeMe : x:int -> int
> > cubeMe 9;;
val it : int = 729
```

Any command-line input or output is written as follows:

```
square 10;;
^^^^^^

error FS0039: The value or constructor 'square' is not defined
```

New terms and **important words** are shown in bold. Words that you see on the screen, for example, in menus or dialog boxes, appear in the text like this: "When this function is executed in **F# interactive**, you can immediately see the results upon invocation as in the following screenshot."

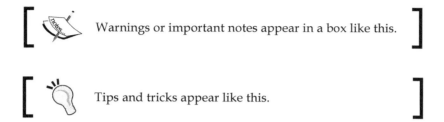

Warnings or important notes appear in a box like this.

Tips and tricks appear like this.

Reader feedback

Feedback from our readers is always welcome. Let us know what you think about this book—what you liked or disliked. Reader feedback is important for us as it helps us develop titles that you will really get the most out of.

To send us general feedback, simply e-mail feedback@packtpub.com, and mention the book's title in the subject of your message.

If there is a topic that you have expertise in and you are interested in either writing or contributing to a book, see our author guide at www.packtpub.com/authors.

Customer support

Now that you are the proud owner of a Packt book, we have a number of things to help you to get the most from your purchase.

Downloading the example code

You can download the example code files from your account at http://www.packtpub.com for all the Packt Publishing books you have purchased. If you purchased this book elsewhere, you can visit http://www.packtpub.com/support and register to have the files e-mailed directly to you. The GitHub repository for the code files are also available at https://github.com/adnanmasood/Learning-fsharp.

Errata

Although we have taken every care to ensure the accuracy of our content, mistakes do happen. If you find a mistake in one of our books—maybe a mistake in the text or the code—we would be grateful if you could report this to us. By doing so, you can save other readers from frustration and help us improve subsequent versions of this book. If you find any errata, please report them by visiting http://www.packtpub.com/submit-errata, selecting your book, clicking on the **Errata Submission Form** link, and entering the details of your errata. Once your errata are verified, your submission will be accepted and the errata will be uploaded to our website or added to any list of existing errata under the Errata section of that title.

To view the previously submitted errata, go to https://www.packtpub.com/books/content/support and enter the name of the book in the search field. The required information will appear under the **Errata** section.

Piracy

Piracy of copyrighted material on the Internet is an ongoing problem across all media. At Packt, we take the protection of our copyright and licenses very seriously. If you come across any illegal copies of our works in any form on the Internet, please provide us with the location address or website name immediately so that we can pursue a remedy.

Please contact us at copyright@packtpub.com with a link to the suspected pirated material.

We appreciate your help in protecting our authors and our ability to bring you valuable content.

Questions

If you have a problem with any aspect of this book, you can contact us at questions@packtpub.com, and we will do our best to address the problem.

1
Embrace the Truth

"Object oriented programming makes code understandable by encapsulating moving parts. Functional programming makes code understandable by minimizing moving parts."

– Michael Feathers

The history of functional programming can be traced back to the Church and Rosser's original work on Lambda Calculus in 1936 and yet, the concepts and implementation of this important programming paradigm are somehow limited to academia while its object-oriented and imperative counterpart dominates the industry. Good news is, this trend is changing fast! With the functional paradigm support in modern programming languages, such as Scala, Clojure, F#, Ruby, and to some extent, the omnipresent JavaScript, the benefits of functional programming are being realized. The increased use of some classical functional languages, such as OCaml, Erlang, Scheme, and Lisp in high-concurrency environments has led to realization of the functional advantages of brevity, terseness, scalability and performance.

In this chapter, we will cover everything that a hobbyist F# developer, who is just starting his/her adventure in functional programming, needs to know in order to be able to follow the discussion through rest of the book. We will begin with a short explanation of F# language's rather special role in the functional programming world, and will explain why it isn't strictly a functional programming language. Throughout the book, and in this chapter particularly, we will address the historic sketches of functional languages and their predecessors. We will discuss F# language's roots in ML, the context in which F# works, that is, running on top of .NET stack, compiled to IL, utilizing BCL, and the hybrid nature of the languages. You will see several new terms used in this and the following chapters; these terms will have a cursory definition, but will be elaborated on as we discuss these topics in detail during subsequent chapters.

By the end of this chapter, you will be familiar with a brief history of functional programming. With comparative code examples, we will analyze code samples using mutable, and immulatable data structures as well as imperative control flow syntax that will allow you, the reader, to fully understand and embrace the hybrid nature of F#.

In this chapter, we will cover the following topics:

- A brief overview of Functional Programming Paradigm
- Thinking functional — why functional programming matters
- The F# language primer
- Benefits of functional programming and functional data structures
- Code samples comparing imperative and functional styles

Exploring the functional programming paradigm

There is no universally accepted definition of functional programming, and any attempt to do so usually results in seemingly infinite stack overflow/Reddit comment threads, flame-wars, and eventually hate-mail. The following are the most agreed upon attributes of a functional programming language:

- Functions are the first class citizens
- Expressions are preferred over statements
- Immutability is revered; structures and data are transformed
- Functions are pure, that is, without side effects
- Composability of functions to combine and chain output
- Programming constructs such as recursion and pattern matching are frequently used
- Non-strict evaluation is the default paradigm

Like its namesake, the functional programming paradigm uses pure functions, as in mathematical functions, as its core construct. The précis of function as a programming language construct stems from Alonzo Church and J. Barkley Rosser's work on lambda calculus. As in mathematical functions, the imperative in *function based programing* is to avoid state and mutation. Like mathematical functions, one should be able to invoke a function multiple times with no side effects, that is, always get the same answers. This style of programing has deep implementation consequences; a focus on immutable data (and structures) leads to programs written in a declarative manner since data structure cannot be a modified piecemeal.

A function is a static, a well-defined mapping from input values to output values. Functions being the *first class citizens* is an often said but seldom understood concept. A programming construct being first class means it may possess certain attributes, such as:

- It can be named or an identifier can be assigned to it
- It can be passed in as an argument, and returned as a value
- It can hold a value, can be chained, and concatenated

Pure functions offer referential transparency, that is, a function always returns the same value when given the same inputs. Pure functions are not always feasible in real-world scenarios such as when using persistent storage, randomization, performing I/O, and generating unique identifiers. Technically speaking, a time function shouldn't exist in a pure functional programming language. Therefore, pure functional languages such as Haskell use the notion of IO Monads to solve this dogmatic conundrum. Luckily for us, the hybrid (albeit more *practical*) languages such as F# are multi-paradigm and can get around this restriction quite easily.

Thinking functional – why functional programming matters

Maintainability is one of the key non-functional requirements when it comes to code upkeep. Software complexity is a deterrent for feature additions, bug fixes, reusability, and refactoring. A well-structured program is not only easy to maintain, but also easy to debug and reuse. In *Why Functional Programming Matters - Research topics in functional programming*, John Huges argues that modularity is key to effective software maintainability, and modularity means more than mere code segmentation. Decomposing a technology or business problem into smaller segments, and then integrating these smaller problems to build a solution, promotes modular and reusable development practices. Code must be usable before it is reusable; the higher order functions and non-strict (lazy) evaluation of functional programming help build smaller, readable, easily testable, and generic modules.

Functional programing provides abstraction but it is relatively different from the hierarchical facet which we are used to seeing in the object oriented paradigm. In contrast with the object oriented tenet of abstraction, functional abstraction hides how the code executes, and provides a protected logical environment which supports referential transparency, that is, programming without side effects. This lets the developer focus on the results based on the statement provided. Functional code is a declaration that describes the results that a developer is trying to achieve, instead of focusing on the steps to get there.

Functional syntax tends to be less verbose and more terse than its imperative or object oriented counterpart. The terseness keeps KLOC low and often results to the improved developer productivity. In terms of productivity, since functional programming promotes and encourages rapid prototyping, it benefits building and testing out proof of concept implementations. This results in code that has more brevity, is more resilient to change, and has fewer bugs.

Even though this is not strictly a feature of functional programming, several cross-cutting concerns come standard along with most functional programming languages. These include protected environments, pattern matching, tail-call optimization, immutable data structures, and garbage collection.

If you have written multi-threaded code, you'd know that debugging the concurrency issues in a multi-threaded environment is difficult to say the least. Arguably, one of the best features of functional programming is thread safety through immutability. The notion of concurrent collections in modern programming languages has its roots in functional programming. The design and use of immutable data structures prevents the process from running into race conditions and therefore does not present a need for explicit locking, semaphores, and mutex programs. This also helps in parallelization, one of the unrealized promises of functional programming.

In this book, we will discuss these and various other functional programming features in detail, especially in context of F#. As a reader who is potentially familiar with either object oriented or imperative programming, you will enjoy the use of fluent-interface methods, lazy and partial evaluation, currying and memoization, and other unique and interesting concepts that make your life as a developer more fulfilling, and easier too.

A historical primer of F#

With the advent of a multi-paradigm language with functional programming support such as Lisp in 1958 by John McCarthy, the functional paradigm gained mainstream exposure. Due to its multi-paradigm nature, there is a debate around Lisp being a pure functional programming language. However, Scheme, one of the Lisp dialects which didn't appear till 1975, tends to favor the functional style. The salient features of this style includes use of tail recursion and continuations to express control flow.

Furthermore, various other functional languages were developed in academia, mostly in the areas of mathematical sciences for theorem proving. ML (meta-language) by Robin Milner et al of University of Edinburgh (early 1970s) is a prime example of a programming language used to first implement the Hindley–Milner type inference system. This simply typed polymorphic lambda calculus language was later adapted to build StandardML, Caml, and OCaml, unifying functional, OOP, and imperative programming paradigms. Haskell emerged in 1990 by Simon Jones et al as a purely functional programming language. Haskell supports lazy evaluation, non-strict semantics, and strong static typing. Haskell is named after the logician Haskell Curry. Not surprisingly, Currying is the functional approach to deconstructing a tuple into evaluating a sequence of functions. It allows us to deconstruct a function that takes multiple arguments into an equivalent sequence of sub-functions that are evaluated, one argument at a time. We will explore currying further in the book.

F#, a product of Don Syme, and Microsoft Research, surfaced in 2005 as a modern multi-paradigm functional programming language. F# originates from ML and has been influenced by OCaml, C#, Python, Haskell, Scala, and Erlang. F# Software Foundation (FSSF) defines the language as follows:

> *"F# is a mature, open source, cross-platform, functional-first programming language. It empowers users and organizations to tackle complex computing problems with simple, maintainable and robust code."*

With an open source compiler, library, and toolset, F# is a multi-paradigm language for the .NET platform with support for multiple operating systems via Mono. It supports functional, object oriented, imperative, and explorative programming paradigms. Software developers who specialize in Microsoft platform and tools can easily learn to take advantage of this new language's functional and object-oriented features. This allows them to use their existing skills, find new productivity gains, and leverage new programming design approaches that cannot be easily expressed in objects alone.

We will be the first to admit that functional programming can be scary for those accustomed to the object oriented and imperative style of coding. While functional programming can lead to some mind-bending coding, the fundamentals are quite straightforward. If you find yourself *lost in lambdas*, rest assured that it takes everyone some time to master these expressions. Even though the primary focus of this book is not F# programming but rather data structures, we will start by introducing some of the F# language tenets to help get the reader up-to-speed.

The syntactical terseness of a functional language like F# can have an adverse effect on the reader; since functional programming is characterized by its concise coding style, brevity, and explicit modeling, this can be hard for those familiar with the verbose algorithmic style of OO and imperative languages. Rest assured, F# also offers a rich set of object oriented features and its integration with other .NET languages such as C#.NET and VB.NET is nearly seamless.

The Hello World example

No book is complete without some quintessential Hello World examples. So here it is:

```
printfn "Hello World";;
```

Yes, this is all you need. Notice the terseness, simplicity, and lack of clutter. Now let's run this in the F# interactive environment. In order to run it, you would need to have ";;" at the end of the statement. We will provide more details on this interactive environment setup later in *Chapter 2, Now Lazily Get Over It, Again.*

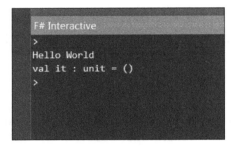

This is the response that you see when you run the preceding line of code. It is a minimal viable example; however these attributes of simplicity, terseness, and simplification extend beyond HelloWorld samples as you will see.

Let's look at a simple function, square. You can write a function in F# as follows:

```
let square = fun n -> n * n
```

Or you can write it in a simpler syntax like the next one. Notice the first-class citizenship in action here:

```
let square n = n * n
```

When this function is executed in **F# interactive**, you can immediately see the results upon invocation as in the following screenshot:

```
F# Interactive
val square : n:int -> int

> square 4
;;
val it : int = 16
>
```

A brief F# language primer

Even though this book is not intended to be an absolute beginner's primer to F#, if you are new to F# there are certain language fundamentals you must know in order to maximize your learning from this book. Following is a quick F# refresher on basic language constructs, keywords, and salient syntactical features that you will find useful during the course of reading this book Several of these items, especially those related to data-structures, are discussed in greater detail in the following chapters. You can download all these examples and source code from the book GitHub repository at https://github.com/adnanmasood/Learning-fsharp.

F# is a statically typed language, that is, types of the variables are known at compile time. Like all other static type languages, F# uses a type inference to resolve the variable type. F# comes with standard data types such as byte, sbyte, int16, uint16, int, uint, int64, uint64, native int, unsigned native int, float or double, float32, decimal, and bignum (System.Numerics.BigInteger). A few simple declarations with appropriate suffixes can be seen as follows:

```
let byte b = 10uy
let sbyte sb = -128y
let int16 i = -100s
let uint16 ui = 100us
let int = -42
let uint = 0x42u
let int64 = 238900L
let uint64 = 2,660,000,000UL
let float f = 3.14159265359
let double db = 2.718281828459045
let float32 f32 = 2.7182818
let decimal d = 3.1415926535897932384626433
let bignum gogol = 10I ** 100
let string = "nà, méi guānxi"
```

Similar to standard CLR data types, F# also uses the standard mathematical operators such as $+-*/,\%\,(modulus)\,and\,**and\,(power)$. Logical operators *such as* $\&\&\,(and)\,||\,(or)\,and\,!(not)$ are supported along with mathematical functions such as $abs, ceil, exp, floor, log, sqrt, cos, sin, tan, and\,pown$. A detailed F# language reference, including Symbol and Operator Reference, can be found at `http://msdn.microsoft.com/en-us/library/dd233228.aspx`.

At this time, we would also like to briefly introduce you to one of the highly useful features of F# IDE, the REPL. **REPL (Read–Eval–Print Loop)** is an interactive language shell to take expression inputs, evaluate, and provide output to the users. REPL allows developers to interact with the language easily and to invoke and test expressions in real-time before writing the entire program. **FSI (F Sharp Interactive)** is the REPL implementation in F#. You will read more about installing and configuring FSI in *Chapter 2*, *Now Lazily Get Over It, Again*. For now you can use the command line version of FSI by invoking it directly in a console:

```
C:\Program Files\Microsoft F#\v4.0\fsi.exe
```

You can also use the `#help;;` directive to list other directives inside FSI.

You will see the `let` binding being used quite frequently for declaring variables, functions, and so on. Functions put functions in functional programming and hence, they are ubiquitous. Technically speaking, F# doesn't have any statements, it only has expressions. The following is a simple example of a function:

```
let cubeMe x = x * x * x;;
```

Instead of explicitly returning a value, F# uses a succinct syntax of returning the value of the expression last evaluated.

```
val cubeMe : x:int -> int
> > cubeMe 9;;
val it : int = 729
```

Recursive functions are defined using the keyword `rec`. Here is a simple implementation of a recursive Fibonacci function:

```
let rec fib n =
  if n <= 2 then 1
  else fib (n - 1) + fib (n - 2)
```

The preceding code for the Fibonacci method takes one parameter as an input. However, a function can have more than one parameters following the same code.

```
let Mult x y = x * y ;;
```

Type inference in F# is an important construct to remember. For instance, in the case of the multiplication function in the preceding line of code, F# assumes the type inference of the arguments as int. A hint can be provided to specify the appropriate data type.

```
let Mult (x: float) (y: float) = x * y ;;
```

Nested or anonymous functions are now commonplace in languages such as C# and Java. These are the special functions that reside inside another function and are not visible from an outside scope. For instance, refer to the following code snippet:

```
let areaOfCircle r =
  let square r = r * r
  System.Math.PI * square r;;
```

However the preceding function will fail upon execution without a hint. We will see the following error on screen:

```
error FS0001: This expression was expected to have type    float      but
here has type    int
```

But the same method will work just fine if the specified data type is passed as float.

```
> areaOfCircle 8.0;;
val it : float = 201.0619298
```

Moreover, you cannot call the inner function directly. That is why the direct call to the square method will return the following error:

```
square 10;;
^^^^^^

error FS0039: The value or constructor 'square' is not defined
```

The conditionals are fundamental to any programming language. F# provides a great pattern-matching scheme along with traditional if...else expressions. The following is a simple if...else check:

```
let Mod10 n =
  if n % 10 = 0 then
    printfn "Number ends in 0"
  else
    printfn "Number does not end in zero";;
```

The print expression will return a value. You can also see the use of elif which is used as a shortcut for else if.

Tuples are now part of a standard CLR system, but most of us remember the struggle before tuples. Tuples are the containers for potentially different types, as seen in the following code:

```
let t = ("cats", "dogs", System.Math.PI, 42, "C#", "Java");;
val t : string * string * float * int * string * string =
  ("cats", "dogs", 3.141592654, 42, "C#", "Java")
```

Speaking of collections, arrays in F# are mutable, fixed-sized sequences. Arrays are fixed in size and zero-indexed, with the elements encapsulated within [| ... |] and separated by a semi-colon.

```
let GuardiansOfGalaxy = [| "Peter Quill"; "Gamora"; "Drax"; "Groot";
  "Rocket"; "Ronan"; "Yondu Udonta"; "Nebula"; "Korath"; "Corpsman
  Dey";"Nova Prime";"The Collector";"Meredith Quill" |]
```

The individual elements of the array can be accessed as follows:

```
let iAmGroot = GuardiansOfGalaxy.[4];
val iAmGroot : string = "Rocket"
```

This also applies to the strings where you can access an individual element of a string as follows:

```
let str = "Lǎo péngyǒu, nǐ kànqǐlái hěn yǒu jīngshén."
printfn "%c" str.[9]
```

Arrays can be created using ranges as follows:

```
let OneToHundred = [|1..100|];;
```

They can be sliced using index (arrays are zero base indexed) as seen in the following code:

```
let TopThree = OneToHundred.[0..2];;
```

Functions in F# can be applied partially; it gets interesting here. A simple add function can be defined as follows:

```
let add x y = x + y;;
```

We can apply it partially to make it add 10 every time. Therefore, the following statement:

```
(add 10) 4;;
```

This can be bound as a method name, or a closure to be exact as seen here:

```
let Add10 = add 10;
val Add10 : (int -> int)
```

This can be explicitly called like the original method, allowing us to compose complex methods using the basic ones. Here, Add10 is a closure that takes one argument and adds 10 to it as seen in the following code:

```
Add10 42
>
val it : int = 52
```

Closures are functionally defined as *a first-class function with free variables that are bound in the lexical environment*. In F#, functions are first class members of the programming society; closures encapsulate an environment for pre-bound variables and create a code block. This way we can pre-define some arguments (in this case, 10). Closure promotes reuse and helps in building complex functions from simpler ones.

With functions as the first class citizens, in F# we can create higher order functions, that is, functions upon functions. Higher order functions operate by taking a function as an argument, or by returning a function. Following are two simple functions:

```
let increament n = n + 1
let divideByTwo n = n / 2
```

Now we will define a higher order function which applies function upon function:

```
let InvokeThrice n (f:int->int) = f(f(f(n)))
```

Now we will use the InvokeThrice function, which will apply the function upon itself three times as defined in the preceding line of code:

```
let res = InvokeThrice 6 increament
>
val res : int = 9
```

In this example, you witnessed the amazing power of declaring functions. A similar approach can be applied to division as follows:

```
let res = InvokeThrice 80 divideByTwo
>
val res : int = 10
```

In the preceding syntax for the `InvokeThrice` function, you will notice the use of a lambda expression. Lambda expressions are ubiquitous in functional programming. In reality, these expressions are syntactic sugar (directives, shortcuts, or a terse way of defining something) to declare anonymous methods. A lambda expression is created using the `fun` keyword, that is, function, followed by arguments which are supposed to be passed to the function. This function declaration is then followed by the lambda arrow operator `->` and the lambda expression which defines the body of the function. For example, instead of passing the function, I can pass the lambda expression during the `InvokeThrice` invocation to apply exponential operation (power 3).

```
let InvokeThrice n (f:double->double) = f(f(f(n)))
let x = InvokeThrice 2.0 (fun n -> n ** 3.0)
```

```
val x : double = 134217728.0
```

Another frequently used F# operator is pipelining | >, which allows us to push arguments onto functions. For example, check the following `cubeMe` method:

```
let cubeMe x = x * x * x;;
```

The preceding method can also be called as `cubeMe` 3 or 3 | > `cubeMe`.

The results will be the same. The pipelining operator allows us to do chaining such as:

```
2 |> cubeMe |> cubeMe |> cubeMe
> val it : int = 134217728
```

This comes in handy when you build functional composites.

Mapping is a frequently used operation in functional programming. Map applies functions on a collection, and displays output as a new list, based on the result of this function. For arrays, F# provides a built-in operation called `map`. The `map` operation takes two arguments—a function and an array of elements. For example, refer to the following array of integers:

```
let nums = [|0..99|]
```

```
val nums : int [] =
  [|0; 1; 2; 3; 4; 5; 6; 7; 8; 9; 10; 11; 12; 13; 14; 15; 16; 17; 18;
  //snip
  97; 98; 99|]
```

The following is the mapping function that will square all the elements in the array, and return a new array:

```
let squares =
  nums
  |> Array.map (fun n -> n * n)
```

When you run the square method on `nums`, you get the following output:

```
val squares : int [] =
  [|0; 1; 4; 9; 16; 25; 36; 49; 64; 81; 100; 121; 144; 169; 196; 225;
256;
//snip
  8649; 8836; 9025; 9216; 9409; 9604; 9801|]
```

The opposite of the map operation is the fold operation. You can think of the folding operations as aggregations. As seen in the preceding code snippet, map takes a collection of arrays and generates another collection. However, the folding operation takes a collection of arrays as input and returns a single object.

For example, in the next statement, `Array.fold` takes three arguments — a function, an initial value for the accumulator, and an array. It sums up the squares of all the three parameters and returns the output:

```
let sum = Array.fold(fun acc n ->  acc + n ) 0 squares
```

```
> val sum : int = 328350
```

Along with map and fold, filtering is another operation which comes in handy to select and filter elements based on a condition (predicate). In the following example, `Array.filter` takes an array of last names and folders them based on the length. Any last name longer than 6 characters will be classified as a long name.

```
let castNames = [| "Hofstadter"; "Cooper"; "Wolowitz"; "Koothrappali";
"Fowler"; "Rostenkowski";  |]

let longNames = Array.filter (fun (name: string) -> name.Length > 6)
castNames
```

The output will be as follows:

```
val longNames : string [] =
  [|"Hofstadter"; "Wolowitz"; "Koothrappali"; "Rostenkowski"|]
```

Similar to map, which applies a function on a collection, a zipping function takes two collections and combines them. In the following example we have two lists:

```
let firstNames = [| "Leonard"; "Sheldon"; "Howard"; "Penny"; "Raj";
"Bernadette"; "Amy" |]
let lastNames = [| "Hofstadter"; "Cooper"; "Wolowitz"; "";
"Koothrappali"; "Rostenkowski"; "Fowler" |]
```

A zip operation when applied on the array returns their full names:

```
let fullNames = Array.zip(firstNames) lastNames
```

Last but not the least, another salient feature of F# language is Lazy or delayed evaluation. These lazy expressions only get evaluated when forced, or when a value is required to be returned. The value then gets memoized (a fancy functional name for caching), and is returned on future recalls. The following is a simple divide method:

```
let divide x y =
  printfn "dividing %d by %d" x y
  x / y
val divide : x:int -> y:int -> int
```

When you invoke the method with the Lazy keyword, the output shows that the value does not get created right away.

```
let answer = lazy(divide 8 2)
val answer : Lazy<int> = Value is not created.
```

However, this can be changed by forcing the results by calling answer.Force():

```
printfn "%d" (answer.Force())
```

```
> dividing 8 by 2
4
val it : unit = ()
```

Now upon force invocation, you would see the value was evaluated by calling the function and therefore you also see dividing 8 by 2 getting printed on the FSI console. Upon consecutive calls such as

```
printfn "%d" (answer.Force())
```

The output would be as follows:

```
4
val it : unit = ()
```

You would not see dividing 8 by 2 getting printed on the FSI console because the value has been computed and memoized. Collections such as sequence are lazy by default, which you will learn in subsequent chapters.

This concludes our whirlwind introduction to the F# programming language; if you are new to F#, you should revise this section a couple of times and run this in the interactive environment to gain familiarity with these fundamental language constructs.

Syntactical similarities and differences

Let's expand upon the preceding example and compare the syntactical differences between F# and C# through another simple example, the sum of a square method. A shorter and elegant looking functional syntax follows:

```
let square x = x * x
let sumOfSquares n = [1..n] |> List.map square |> List.sum
```

Here you see the use of one of F#'s celebrated operators, that is, the |> pipe forward operator. It essentially performs piping operations by passing the results from left the side of the function to the right side, and can be concatenated.

Running this program in F# the interactive console yields the following results for

sumOfSquares 2

and

sumOfSquares 3

respectively:

```
F# Interactive
Microsoft (R) F# Interactive version 12.0.21005.1
Copyright (c) Microsoft Corporation. All Rights Reserved.

For help type #help;;

>

val square : x:int -> int
val sumOfSquares : n:int -> int
val it : int = 5

>

val square : x:int -> int
val sumOfSquares : n:int -> int
val it : int = 14
```

The sum of the squares method in C# looks something like this:

```
public class SumOfSquares
{
  public static int CalculateSquaresSum(int n)
  {
    var sum = 0;
    for (var i = 1; i <= n; i++)
    {
      sum += Square(i);
    }
    return sum;
  }
  public static int Square(int x)
  {
    return x * x;
  }
}
```

Again, the C# version is quite verbose and can be made more functional by using LINQ as seen next:

```
public static int SquaresSum(int n)
{
  return Enumerable.Range(1, n)
  .Select(i => i * i)
  .Sum();
}
```

This can be further reduced to the following code:

```
public static int SquaresSum(int n)
{
  return Enumerable.Range(1, n)
  .Sum(i => i * i);
}
```

In this case, `IEnumerable` is used along with a `Select` filter, which sums up the results. Numbers from a sequence are each squared and aggregated into a sum.

Project Euler provides a series of mathematical and programming problems that can be solved using programming languages of your choice. Following is problem #1 from Project Euler:

> *If we list all the natural numbers below 10 that are multiples of 3 or 5, we get 3, 5, 6 and 9. The sum of these multiples is 23 Find the sum of all the multiples of 3 or 5 below 1000.*

An F# solution to this problem can be written as follows:

```
let total = [1..999] |> List.map (fun i -> if i % 5 = 0 || i % 3 = 0
then i else 0) |> List.sum
```

In this case we operate on 1-999, chain the operator with map to perform a modulus operation, and then sum up the results. An alternate approach is to use a filter that categorizes the results and provides a collection to perform a sum on. This approach can be listed as follows:

```
let total = [1..999] |> List.filter (fun i -> i % 5 = 0 || i % 3 = 0)
|> List.sum
```

The solution in C# following the same algorithm results in a verbose listing as seen here:

```
public static int CalcSumOfMultiples()
{
  int result = 0;
  for (int i = 1; i < 1000; i++)
  {
    if ((i % 3) == 0 || (i % 5) == 0)
    {
      result += i;
    }
  }
  return result;
}
```

This C# code can be LINQ'ified to a more terse syntax as follows:

```
var total = Enumerable.Range(1, 999).Select(x => x % 3 == 0 || x % 5
== 0 ? x : 0).Sum();
```

Another better way of doing this can be seen in the next code listing:

```
var total = Enumerable.Range(1, 999).Sum(x => x%3 == 0 || x%5 == 0 ? x
: 0);
```

The F# solutions of Project Euler problems, to further help understand algorithms and data structures can be found at https://github.com/adnanmasood/Euler.Polyglot.

Benefits of using F# over C#

And now on to the language wars!

A common inquiry among seasoned C# developers is, "What is the benefit of using F#? Or to word it differently, why do I need to learn a new language when I can perform the same tasks in the language I already know and love?"

A good analogy is LaTeX versus Microsoft Word. You may have used LaTeX for typesetting. For complicated tasks, Word becomes *too complex or even unusable*. Marko Pinteric explains why you would want to use LaTeX instead of Word with the following graph:

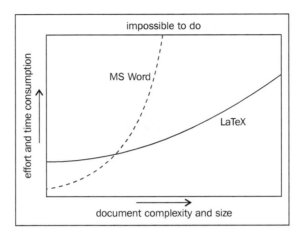

Complexity and learning curve. Using LaTeX on Windows by Marko Pinteric (www.pinteric.com/miktex.html)

The same applies to F#. Functional programming does have a learning curve but it equips you with the tools needed to go further in algorithmic software development. This eventually leads to the argument of general benefits of functional programming over imperative and object oriented languages.

Using functional programming with F#, one can arguably formulate and design solutions in an easier, more effective manner, especially if these problems pertain to the algorithmic domain. As a functional language, F# facilitates keeping the problem closer to their definition in a concise and terse manner. From the testability perspective, the resulting code becomes less error-prone due to its powerful type system, intuitive recursive representation of algorithms, and built-in immutability. Data structure immutability is especially helpful in the case of multi-threaded scenarios. This is, in essence, due to built-in data type immutability.

The specific F# advantages include the following:

1. Interoperability with the .NET CLR languages.
2. Ease of asynchronous programming, intuitive use of `async {}` expressions.
3. Full Visual Studio .NET IDE integration with compiler and debugger support.
4. Suitability for writing domain-specific languages and compilers.

5. Improved performance, scalability, and reduced maintenance cost due to enhanced testability and terseness.

6. Language extensibility features such as units of measurements, record types, and language-oriented programming support.

Any functional language in general, and F# in particular, is not a silver bullet and shouldn't be treated as one. For UI centric and other applications of highly stateful nature, C# and other imperative .NET languages are a better fit than a functional programming language. Having said that, if you are a quant, who is writing high frequency trading algorithms in F#, or a rewriting to improve an existing VWAP implementation, you will be delighted to know that you can easily expose the F# functionality using your server-side C# WCF libraries. However, since you can have F# and C# together in one .NET solution, it is easy to combine the benefits of both languages and use as needed.

Summary

To summarize, F# provides the combined benefits of succinct syntax, immutable types, interoperability, efficiency, concurrency, and scalability — an impressive list. Functional programming has a well established repertoire as an efficient way of modeling complex problems in its respective mathematical form. F#, as a modern multi-paradigm language, is quite practical for enterprises, and gives developers and software architects an excellent reason to start using functional programming in their projects.

We recommend reading *Functional thinking: Why functional programming is on the rise*, by Neal Ford, who is a software architect at ThoughtWorks, at `www.ibm.com/developerworks/library/j-ft20/` as a follow up reading to reinforce some of the concepts discussed in this chapter.

In this chapter, we have covered an introduction to functional programming paradigm along with some key syntactical elements of the F# programming language. We have established the notion of thinking in functional style and explained why functional programming matters? We also elaborated on the benefits of functional programming and functional data structures along with code based comparisons of imperative and functional paradigms.

In the next chapter, we will gain further knowledge about the F# tooling, syntax, and semantics of the language and learn to write some programs using F#.

2
Now Lazily Get Over It, Again

"Ah yes, Haskell. Where all the types are strong, all the men carry arrows, and all the children are above average."

– marked trees (on the city of Haskell)

The perceived adversity of functional programming is overly exaggerated; the essence of this paradigm is to explicitly recognize and enforce the referential transparency. The previous chapter was an attempt to convince you about how amazing functional programming is; you saw some examples and read about some promised features but understandably, you are still little bit skeptical. This chapter will prepare you to delve into the F# fundamentals that we are going to utilize later.

 We will see how to set up the tooling for Visual Studio 2013 and for F# 3.1, the currently available version of F# at the time of writing. We will review the F# 4.0 preview features by the end of this project.

After we get the tooling sorted out, we will review some simple algorithms; starting with recursion with typical a Fibonacci sequence and Tower of Hanoi, we will perform lazy evaluation on a quick sort example. By the end of this chapter, you will be able to set up a development environment utilizing recursion as a major technique of functional algorithm designs, learn using memoization to cache intermediate results, and apply lazy evaluation in order to skip the unnecessary overhead of full execution.

In this chapter, we will cover the following topics:

- Setting up Visual Studio and F# compiler to work together
- Setting up the environment and running your F# programs
- Implementing a Fibonacci sequence using recursion
- Implementing Tower of Hanoi using recursion
- Applying lazy evaluation for quick sort

Setting up the IDE

As developers, we love our **IDEs (Integrated Development Environments)** and Visual Studio.NET is probably the best IDE for .NET development; no offense to eclipse bloatware Luna. From the open source perspective, there has been a recent major development in making the .NET framework available as open source and on Mac and Linux platforms. Microsoft announced a pre-release of F# 4.0 in Visual Studio 2015 Preview and it will be available as part of the full release.

To install and run F#, there are various options available for all platforms, sizes, and budgets. For those with a fear of commitments, there is the online interactive version of TryFsharp at `http://www.tryfsharp.org/` where you can code in the browser.

For Windows users, you have a few options. Until VS.NET 2015 comes out, you can try out the freely available Visual Studio Community 2013 or a Visual Studio 2013 trial edition, with *trial* being the keyword. The trial editions include Ultimate, Premium, and Professional versions. The free community edition IDE can be downloaded from `https://www.visualstudio.com/en-us/news/vs2013-community-vs.aspx` and the trial editions can be downloaded from `http://www.visualstudio.com/downloads/download-visual-studio-vs`.

Alternatively, there are express editions available at no cost. Visual Studio Express 2013 for Windows Desktop Web editions can be downloaded from `http://www.visualstudio.com/downloads/download-visual-studio-vs#d-express-windows-desktop`.

F# support is built into Visual Studio; the Visual F# tools package the latest updates to the F# compiler: interactive, runtime, and Visual Studio integration. F# support comes with Visual Studio. However, the F# team releases regular updates in the form of F# tools. The tools can be downloaded from `www.microsoft.com/en-us/download/details.aspx?id=44011`.

The F# tools contain the F# command-line compiler (`fsc.exe`) and F# Interactive (`fsi.exe`), which are the easiest way to get started with F#. The `fsi.exe` compiler can be found in `C:\Program Files (x86)\Microsoft SDKs\F#\<version>\Framework\<version>\`.

The <version> placeholder in the preceding path is substituted by your .NET version installed. If you just want to use the F# compiler and tools from the command line, you can download the .NET framework 4.5 or above from https://www.microsoft.com/en-in/download/details.aspx?id=30653. You will also need the Windows SDK for associated dependencies, which can be downloaded from http://msdn.microsoft.com/windows/desktop/bg162891.

Alternatively, Tsunami is the free IDE for F# that you can download from http://tsunami.io/download.html and use to build applications. CloudSharper by IntelliFactory is in beta but shows promise as a web-based IDE. For more information regarding CloudSharper, refer to http://cloudsharper.com/.

In this book, we will be using **Visual Studio 2013 Professional Edition** and FSI (F# interactive) but you can either use the trial or Express edition, or the FSI command line to run the examples and exercises.

Your first F# project

Going through installation screens and showing how to click **Next** would be discourteous to our reader's intelligence. Therefore we will skip step-by-step installation for other more verbose texts. Let's start with our first F# project in Visual Studio.

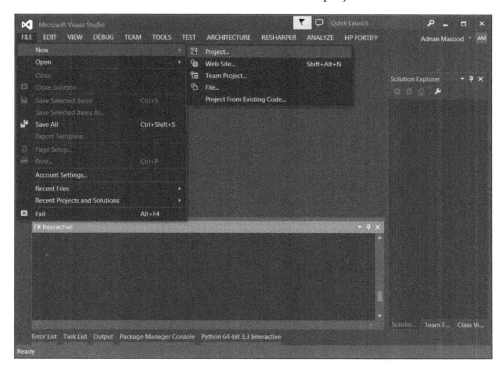

In the preceding screenshot, you can see the **F# interactive** window at the bottom. Here we have selected **FILE | New | Project** because we are attempting to open a new project of F# type. There are a few project types available, including console applications and F# library. For ease of explanation, let's begin with a **Console Application** as shown in the next screenshot:

Alternatively, from within Visual Studio, we can use FSharp Interactive. **FSharp Interactive** (**FSI**) is an effective tool for testing out your code quickly. You can open the FSI window by selecting **View | Other Windows | F# Interactive** from the Visual Studio IDE as shown in the next screenshot:

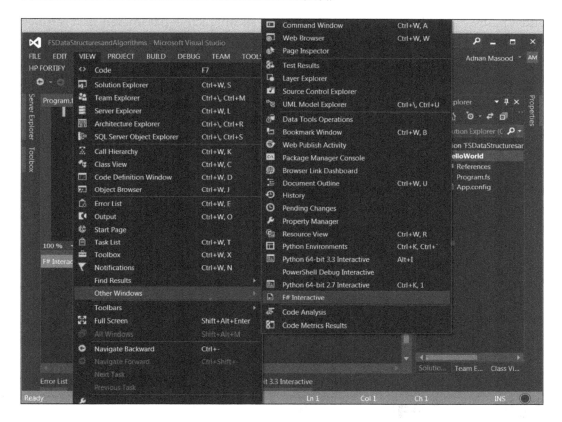

FSI lets you run code from a console which is similar to a shell. You can access the FSI executable directly from the location at `c:\Program Files (x86)\Microsoft SDKs\F#\<version>\Framework\<version>\`.

FSI maintains session context, which means that the constructs created earlier in the FSI are still available in the later parts of code.

The `FsiAnyCPU.exe` executable file is the 64-bit counterpart of F# interactive; Visual Studio determines which executable to use based on the machine's architecture being either 32-bit or 64-bit. You can also change the F# interactive parameters and settings from the **Options** dialog as shown in the following screenshot:

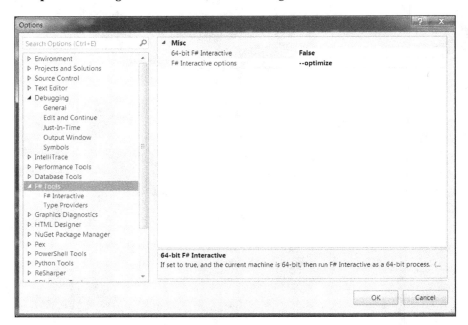

Talk is cheap, show me some code

In the next screenshot, you will see a simple print statement (`Hello World`). This statement is executed in the interactive environment by highlighting the statement (you do not need to highlight [`<EntryPoint>`]) and then pressing *Alt + Enter*. You will see the output of the command in the FSI window as shown in the following screenshot:

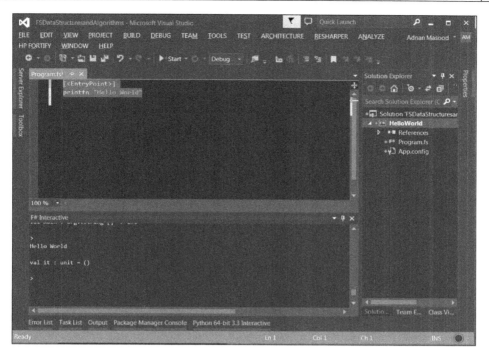

You can also run the program from the context menu by selecting the code to execute and right-clicking in the code window to launch the context menu, followed by selecting the **Execute in Interactive** option. The following screenshot shows the context menu:

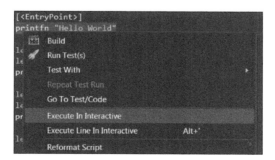

F# interactive provides a large set of features that we will use throughout this book. If you are interested in knowing more about FSI, please refer to the FSI Reference on MSDN at http://msdn.microsoft.com/en-us/library/dd233175.aspx.

Now that we have run our first program, let's do some Math. is The F# `let` statement is used to bind an identifier, which can be a value or a function. In the following screenshot, we define a `multiply` function that will take two variables as arguments, and return their product.

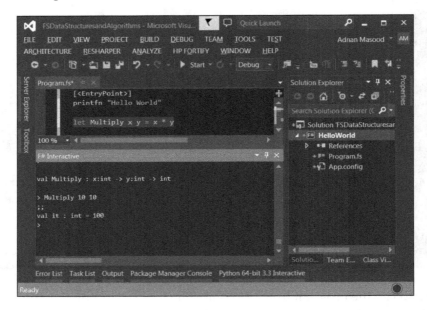

You will now start to realize the terseness of the F# syntax; the missing parenthesis, lack of type declarations, and no return statement! Upon executing the line of code by selecting it and pressing *Alt + Enter* (or selecting and running it from the context menu as shown in the preceding screenshot), we can now execute the function.

We typed `Multiply 10 10` in the FSI window, followed by `;;` (a terminating token, required only in interactive mode), and saw the result (along with the resulting type) as `100`. This is the power of REPL or the Console Prompt that allows you to run commands in an interactive manner.

Because we don't need much code ceremony and boilerplate bloat, it is simple and efficient to build and execute algorithms in F#.

Before we proceed further, let's quickly examine F# project types in Visual Studio which are as follows:

- **Console Application**: This creates command line applications
- **F# Library**: This creates an F# library; it can be used from other programming languages

- **Tutorial**: This is a tutorial walk-through; it is highly recommended for beginners

- **Portable Library (legacy and new)**: This is a portable library for .NET 4.5 and Windows Store

- **Silverlight Library**: This is an F# Silverlight library to be used in Silverlight applications

Since the focus of this text is mainly on data structures and algorithms, we will concentrate on console applications and F# libraries. Also for F# File types, the scripts use the file extension `.fsx` or `.fsscript` while the source code files use the `.fs` extension. F# has three different types of environments namely interactive, scripting, and compiled environments. We will see more, as we work through examples.

To understand recursion, you must understand recursion

Recursion is an integral part of functional programming. The emphasis on recursive methods in functional programming is mainly due to the reason that you don't need a mutable state, hence making it simple and straightforward to semantically define a term. Due to this prevalence of recursion as a functional construct and its semantic differences from other functional programming languages like Haskell, F# provides a keyword for recursion that is, `rec`. This is how you define a recursive function:

```
let rec recursive-function-identifier parameter-list =
    recursive-function-body
```

Factorial is usually a simple example to begin explaining how recursion works. To jog your memory, the factorial of n is the product of all the numbers from $1...n$, that is,

$$n! = n \times (n-1) \times (n-2)...\times 3 \times 2 \times 1$$

Hence the output will be as follows:

$$5! = 1 \times 2 \times 3 \times 4 \times 5 = 120$$

Since F# is a multi-paradigm language, let's first try to solve this using an imperative approach as seen in the next screenshot:

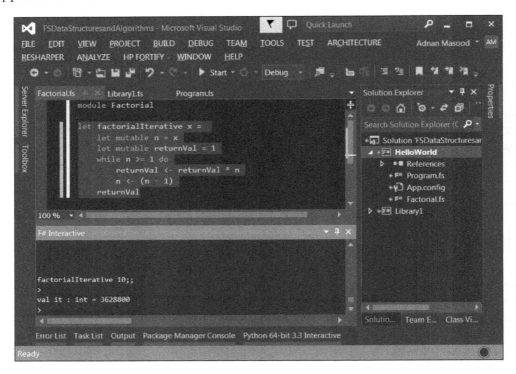

The iterative implementation of a factorial looks like follows:

```
let factorialIterative x =
  let mutable n = x
  let mutable returnVal = 1
  while n >= 1 do
    returnVal <- returnVal * n
    n <- (n - 1)
  returnVal
```

Downloading the example code

You can download the example code files for all Packt books you have purchased from your account at http://www.packtpub.com. If you purchased this book elsewhere, you can visit http://www.packtpub.com/support and register to have the files e-mailed directly to you. The GitHub repository for the code files are also available at https://github.com/adnanmasood/Learning-fsharp.

In the preceding code snippet, you will see a few new keywords. It is important to understand that this is non-idiomatic F#; here we are using the `mutable` keyword, which signifies that the value can be changed. Mutability of a variable is a contentious topic between the purist and pragmatic factions of functional programming. F# allows mutability but also recommends that the scope of mutable variables is kept to a minimum. In the following line of code, if you do not use `mutable`, the assignment will fail:

```
n <- (n - 1)
```

You also see the `while` loop here. Following is a basic `while` syntax:

```
while test-expression do
  body-expression
```

In this iterative example which is very similar to other procedural language implementations, the `while` loop runs through n, decreasing value, multiplying, and accumulating the values in the `returnVal` variable, eventually returning it back. You will also notice that the scope (where the function begins and ends) is maintained through indentation, as compared to C style brackets.

The iterative example just shown is to demonstrate the multi-paradigm nature and flexibility of F#. Now let's do this the right way.

"To iterate is human, to recurse divine."

– L. Peter Deutsch

The simple recursive implementation of a factorial invokes itself (recursively), with a decrement in value of n until it reaches 1.

```
//Recursive
let rec factorial n =
  if n < 1 then 1
  else n * factorial  (n - 1)
```

Here you notice the use of `rec`, the F# recursion keyword, and the recursive calling of the `factorial` method. As shown in the **F# interactive** window in the following screenshot, when the method is invoked, it displays the factorial of the number:

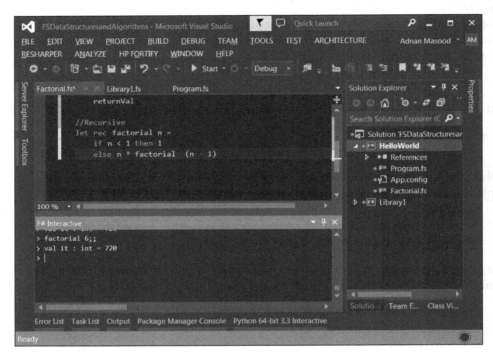

In this simple recursive factorial method, you can see the elegance and simplicity that distinguishes itself from the iterative implementation. However, recursion is not without dangers for large implementations, such as severe performance penalties and stack overflow, and you need to be careful how, when, and where you decide to implement it. This is probably not a concern when developing and trying out new algorithms. First make it work, and then make it fast. Knuth famously said that premature optimization is the root of all evil in programming.

Tail recursion is a good way to minimize stack consumption, and increase speed, as will be seen in the examples shortly.

In many F# examples, you will see the pattern matching syntax being used. If you are just starting out with F#, I would recommend against using it because it may end up confusing you. As it is famously said about Perl, that is it is the only language that looks the same before and after **RSA** encryption, F# syntax matching expressions may end up having the same effect. For instance, the method above can also be written as a pattern matching expression which returns the following equations:

$$n \ when \ n < 1-> 1$$

$$n-> n * factorial\left(n-1\right)$$

The _ operator is the wildcard expression that matches anything and typically comes last as an everything-else clause. The pipe operator is used to match expressions, and to delimit the matching cases.

$$|\left(pattern \ match\right)$$

The following code snippet is a complete listing for the pattern matching idiomatic F# recursive factorial function:

```
let rec factorial_PatternMatching n =
  match n with
  | 0 | 1 -> 1
  | _ -> n * factorial(n-1)
```

Even though the syntax is terse and mathematically sound, this may hinder readability at times. Pragmatically, it is a good idea to use the best judgement in terms of readability, when using the pattern matching statements.

Tail recursion is the optimization applied when the last statement of a function is the recursive call. This eliminates the need for storing the last instruction pointer reference to identify where a function should go to continue execution.

```
//Tail Recursive
let factorial n =
  let rec tailRecFact n accum =
    if n <= 1 then
      accum
    else
      tailRecFact (n - 1) (accum * n)
  tailRecFact n 1
```

By introducing an accumulator variable, we can now accumulate the results and iterate indefinitely, without taking up stack space. The CLR implementation of this method is essentially identical to an iterative `while` loop.

Another approach to implementing a factorial in functional style is to use continuation. Continuation is a functional programing construct; it is essentially a function that is passed to a function to instruct what needs to be done next.

```
// Continutaion based factorial
let factorial n =
  let rec contTailRecFact n f =
    if n <= 1 then
      f ()
    else
      contTailRecFact (n - 1) (fun () -> n * f ())
  contTailRecFact n (fun () -> 1)
```

Similar to the first implementation with the accumulator, in the preceding code you see the `contTailRecFact` method. However, now pass a function instead of passing the accumulator variable.

Higher order functions are another construct used to address the concerns raised due to recursive logic. A more idiomatic list-processing approach is using the `List.fold <'T, 'State>` function. It applies the function to each element of the collection. Several List module functions apply a function to elements. In the case of `fold`, this is done by threading an accumulator argument (state) through the computation. A generic signature of `List.Fold` follows:

```
List.fold : ('State -> 'T -> 'State) -> 'State -> 'T list -> 'State
```

Simplify the implementation to the following:

```
let factorial n = [1..n]
  |> List.fold (*) 1
```

The same approach can be applied in the case of the `List.Reduce` method, which chains the results into the next arguments. It takes two parameters—the function used to reduce two list elements to a single element and the list itself. The reduce signature follows:

```
List.reduce : ('T -> 'T -> 'T) -> 'T list -> 'T

let factorial n = [1..n]
  |> List.reduce (*)
```

The `List.Reduce` method applies the supplied function to each element of the `List`, threading an accumulator argument. The function is applied to the first two elements of the list, which then passes the result to the function, along with the third element. This continues until the final result is computed.

We realize that this is essentially a whirlwind tour of several important functional programming concepts such as continuations, folding/unfolding, tail call optimization and so on. However, the scope of this book limits us from delving into further details. For curious minds, we have provided details to pertinent resources in *Chapter 10, Where to Go Next?*.

Memoization with Fibonacci

Like factorials, **Fibonacci** is another one of those easy-to-explain problem statements that can be used to demonstrate a language's capabilities in a simple and easy to understand manner. A Fibonacci series is written as follows:

$$1,1,2,3,5,8,...$$

It can also be written as a recurrence:

$$F_n = F_{n-1} + F_{n-2}$$

$$F0 = 0$$

$$F1 = 1$$

$$F_n = F_n - 1 + F_n - 2, if \ n > 1$$

$$F_n = F_n + 2 - F_n + 1, if \ n < 0$$

Now that you know what factorials are, a recursive Fibonacci implementation comes very naturally as follows:

```
let rec fibonacci n =
  if n <= 2 then 1
  else fibonacci (n - 1) + fibonacci (n - 2)
```

However, based on the earlier factorial solution, you quickly realize that this is indeed not tail-optimized, and will result in a stack overflow. This is due to pushing of pointers in the stack. Applying the same pattern as for the factorial, by using an external function `fibonacci` and internal recursive function `fibonacci_TailRecursive`, the resulting tail-optimized method can be written as follows:

```
let fibonacci_TailRecursive n =
    let rec fibonacciX (n, x, y) =
        if (n = 0I) then x
        else fibonacciX ((n - 1I), y, (x + y))
    fibonacciX (n, 0I, 1I)
```

Memoization (a fancy name for caching), is another programming optimization technique in which the results from a previous computation are stored for later retrieval when the arguments are presented again. In the case of `fibonacci`, when we reuse the values frequently, it is prudent to use the memoization construct.

Therefore, we introduce a dictionary called `cache` in the code snippet that follows. Also, improving the traditional `if...else`syntax, here we use idiomatic pattern matching in the function. The letter `I` next to the number forces the use of `BigInteger`, which is useful for making large calculations. To reference generic types, you would have to include `System.Numerics` to include the big integer type.

```
open System.Collections.Generic

let rec fibonacci_Generic n =
    let cache = Dictionary<_, _>()
    let rec fibonacciX = function
        | n when n = 0I -> 0I
        | n when n = 1I -> 1I
        | n -> fibonacciX (n - 1I) + fibonacciX (n - 2I)
    if cache.ContainsKey(n) then cache.[n]
    else
        let result = fibonacciX n
        cache.[n] <- result
        result
```

The array syntax in F# is due to its OCaml foundations, and those familiar with C style languages find it odd. Rest assured, `cache.[n]` is the same as `cache[n]` that is used in C/C#, Java, and other C-like languages. When invoking the method, you need to use I next to the number to avoid getting the following exception. The suffix lets FSI infer the right type for invocation:

```
error FS0001: This expression was expected to have type   System.
Numerics.BigInteger    but here has type    int
```

The following screenshot shows the execution of the memorization version of the Fibonacci sequence function. A neat trick to do a "poor man's performance benchmarking" in the interactive window is to use the `#time` directive. As seen in the screenshot , the time taken starts recording when `#time` is executed first, and ends when it is called again, capturing the time taken:

```
> #time
fibonacci 20I
#time
;;
```

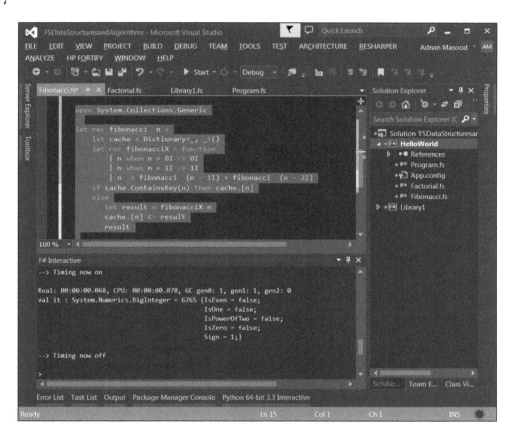

Higher order function passing, memoization, tail recursion, continuations, and a combination of these techniques yield well-designed solutions. Unfortunately, there are no hard and fast rules stating which optimization technique should be used to solve a particular problem. It is usually a trade-off between time, memory consumption, ease of programming, clarity, and data variability.

Towers of Hanoi

Let's review another programming problem called Towers of Hanoi and solve it using F#. The puzzle was invented by a French mathematician, Édouard Lucas, in 1883 and has been heavily cited in programming literature including Ralf Hinze's Functional Pearl: La Tour D'Hanoi (http://www.comlab.ox.ac.uk/ralf.hinze/publications/ICFP09.pdf). The objective of the puzzle is to move the tower from the starting pole to the target pole in the minimum number of steps following two simple rules:

1. Only one top disk is allowed to move to a different pole during an action.

2. A large disk cannot be placed on top of a smaller disk.

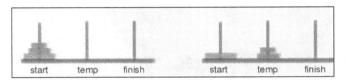

A simple Pascal implementation by Daniel W. Palmer, **TOWERS OF HANOI** in JCSC 12, can easily be implemented in F#. The procedure's pseudo code with the Start, Target (finish) and the Aux (temp) variables is given as follows:

```
procedure Hanoi(n : integer; Start, Aux, Target : char);
begin
    if n > 0 then
    begin
            Hanoi(n-1, Start, Target, Aux);
            writeln('Move ',Start,' to ',Target);
            Hanoi(n-1, Aux, Start, Target);
    end;
end;
```

The F# recursive version, similar to the approach described in the preceding screenshot, will result in following non-idiomatic code, and is shown here for the sake of simplicity and explanation. In the signature, f is the from, x is the intermediate state, t is the to (destination), and n is the number of pegs or disks:

```
let rec TowerOfHanoi f x t n =
  if n > 0 then
    TowerOfHanoi  f t x (n - 1)
    printfn "Move disc from %c to %c" f t
    TowerOfHanoi  x f t (n - 1)
```

When the preceding code is run for the following dataset:

```
TowerOfHanoi 'x' 'y' 'z' 4
```

The resulting steps will be outlined as follows:

```
Move disc from x to y
Move disc from x to z
Move disc from y to z
Move disc from x to y
Move disc from z to x
Move disc from z to y
Move disc from x to y
Move disc from x to z
Move disc from y to z
Move disc from y to x
Move disc from z to x
Move disc from y to z
Move disc from x to y
Move disc from x to z
Move disc from y to z
```

Let's improve upon this approach using idiomatic F#. An elegant OCaml solution described in *Well-Founded Coalgebras*, by Jean-Baptiste Jeannin (http://www.cs.cornell.edu/~kozen/papers/theory.pdf) is described as follows:

```
let rec hanoi n o d t =
  if n = 0 then [ ] else
    (hanoi (n-1) o t d) @ [(o,d)] @ (hanoi (n-1) t d o)
```

Transforming this in F# is fairly easy. The only new thing you'd see here is the use of @ and _ as concatenation, and pattern matching operators used to pass the respective parameters as in the following code snippet. The parameters being passed are n (number of pegs), s (starting location), and f (ending position):

```
let rec TowerOfHanoiRec n s f =
  match n with
  | 0 -> [ ]
  | _ -> let t = (6 - s - f)
    (TowerOfHanoiRec (n-1) s t) @ [ s, f ] @ (TowerOfHanoiRec(n-1) t
f)
```

This, in turn, can be invoked by the following statement:

```
(TowerOfHanoi 2 1 2) |> List.iter (fun pair -> match pair with
  | x, y -> printf "Move the disc from %A to %A\n" x y)
```

As suggested by Marcin Juraszek, the technical reviewer, this can be further shortened to:

```
(TowerOfHanoi 2 1 2) |> List.iter (fun (x,y) -> printf "Move the disc
from %A to %A\n" x y)
```

The following are the results in multiple steps for solving the Towers of Hanoi:

```
Move disc
from 1 to 2
Move disc from 1 to 3
Move disc from 2 to 3
Move disc from 1 to 2
Move disc from 3 to 1
Move disc from 3 to 2
Move disc from 1 to 2
```

Sorting lazily

The functional feature of `lazy` computations in F# allows for delayed evaluations, that is, only compute when needed. This feature improves performance and prevents excessive computations when not needed:

```
let identifier = lazy ( expression )
```

The `lazy` identifier in the preceding code delays the evaluation of an expression or contained code segment. Let's explain this with a simple example as seen in the following screenshot:

When the `lazy` keyword is used, the expression is not evaluated immediately; the computation happens only when requested. This is not the case with a non-lazy expression where the value was calculated and printed right away. The value was evaluated and printed right away, albeit as needed, when we *requested* it as follows:

```
> x.Value
;;
```

```
F# Interactive
> let x = lazy(printfn "Lazy Evaluation"; 2 * 2);;

val x : Lazy<int> = Value is not created.

> x.Value
;;
Lazy Evaluation
val it : int = 4
>
```

Besides these primitive operations, there are more sophisticated data structures such as sequence cache and LazyList which are built using the lazy evaluation constructs. Unfortunately, F# lists are not lazy by default and LazyLists are provided as part of the F# power pack. Let's use our newly found knowledge to implement Quicksort, the classical poster-boy for functional languages. Further details and a complexity analysis of Quicksort are discussed with illuminating details in *Algorithms* by Robert Sedgewick (http://algs4.cs.princeton.edu/23quicksort/).

The Quicksort algorithm has an average case complexity of $O(n \log n)$, that is, logarithmic order, and in the worst case, $O(n^2)$ (quadratic) uses a fairly yet effective pivotal approach with recursion and can be defined as follows:

1. Select a Pivot from the given array.
2. Partition the data into two lists such as, elements with values less than the pivotal element reside in the first list and elements with values greater than the pivot element reside in the second list.
3. Use Quicksort to separately sort both the lists recursively.
4. Combine the first sorted list, the pivot value, and the second sorted list.

A recursive F# implementation of the algorithm, with the list pattern matching operator (::), is used in partitioning to separate the parts of a list. This can be written as follows:

```
let rec quickSort = function
    | [] -> []
    | n::ns -> let lessthan, greaterEqual = List.partition ((>) n) ns
    quickSort lessthan @ n :: quickSort greaterEqual
```

As shown in the following screenshot, when the `quickSort` method is invoked on a list of 10 random numbers, it applies a quick sort and returns a sorted list:

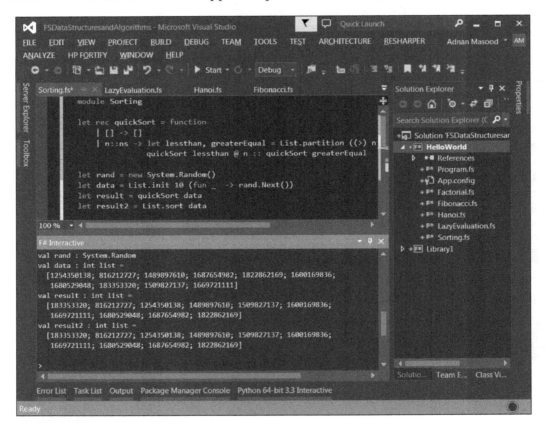

Even though the first implementation is idiomatic and recursive, an improved functional and lazy implementation using sequences is better suited for this beginner-oriented text.

Let's introduce sequence in our original Quicksort implementation. The Haskell inspired functional implementation of Qquicksort is done by Tony Lee and is available on F# snippets at `http://www.fssnip.net/5d`.

```
let rec quickSort_func (pxs:seq<_>) =
  seq {
    match Seq.toList pxs with
    | p::xs -> let lessthan, greaterEqual = List.partition ((>=) p) xs
        yield! quickSort lessthan; yield p; yield! quickSort
greaterEqual
    | _ -> ()
  }
```

Due to the its implementation as a sequence, which is a `lazy` structure, the `take` statement provides a much faster response time. `Sequence.Take` returns the elements of the sequence up to a specified count. The signature is shown as follows:

```
Seq.take : int -> seq<'T> -> seq<'T>
data |> quickSort |> Seq.take 1
```

However, operations that require lengthy evaluation with large computations can take much longer — an example is the one returning the length of a sequence:

```
data |> quickSort |> Seq.length
```

F# 4.0 – new features

With the release of Visual Studio 2015 RC (release candidate), F# 4.0 language and tools updates are now provided. There are various new features added in F# 4.0, including constructors such as first-class functions, metaprogramming support, simplified mutable/ref values, inheritance from types with multiple generic interface, and normalized collections API to name a few apart from supporting fractional exponents such as units of measure. You can find the complete list of features at `http://blogs.msdn.com/b/dotnet/archive/2015/04/29/rounding-out-visual-f-4-0-in-vs-2015-rc.aspx`.

F# 4.0 is also different in another import aspect. As a community-oriented project, three-fourth of contributors are not affiliated with Microsoft. Even the time-honored naming convention of `Microsoft.FSharp` is now optional. It can be omitted when referring to namespaces, modules, and types from the `FSharp.Core` runtime.

Although, there are several significant enhancements in the F# 4.0 language, runtime, and IDE for F#, there are major impacts from the data structures and algorithms perspective. We recommend you to review all the changes—as mentioned in the preceding link —to see the features, such as IDE enhancements, script debugging support, and async extensions to web client in action. Features such as extension properties used as object initializers are now available in F#, which shows Microsoft's commitment to keep F# as a first class citizen in the .NET ecosystem.

Summary

In this chapter, we covered setting up of Visual Studio .NET and F# Compiler to work together with the environment and runtime. We reviewed how you can run your F# programs in IDE and via an interactive REPL shell. We also implemented a Fibonacci sequence and Tower of Hanoi using recursion, and applied lazy evaluation for a quick sort.

In the next chapter, we will gain knowledge about the built-in data structures: array, list, set, and map, and will present their typical use cases. So now, what part of Hindley–Milner type inference algorithm do you not understand?

What's in the Bag Anyway?

The computing scientist's main challenge is not to get confused by the complexities of his own making.

– E. W. Dijkstra

In the previous chapter, we went over the installation of Visual Studio IDE, recursion constructs, and looked at a few basic examples of typical algorithms while implementing it using F#. In this chapter, we will cover built-in data structures: array, list, set, and map, and will present their typical use cases, especially around operations used mostly in functional programming. In this chapter, you will learn how to utilize built-in data structures, and will gain an improved ability to instinctively choose the appropriate data structure (mutable versus persistent) for specific tasks. You will also learn to use typical sorting algorithms (bubble, selection, merge) and towards the end, learn to see how the **Big-O notation** is used to choose between algorithms.

In this chapter, we will cover the following topics:

* Analysis of built-in data structures with distinction between the mutable and persistent ones

* Presentation of common operations on arrays, lists, sets, and maps

* Introduction to list comprehensions, active pattern, and querying (for example, `groupBy`)

* An overview of sorting algorithms with a discussion on Big-O

* Comparing the performance of quicksort versus merge sort in a functional setting

Exploring data structures in F#

Data structures are, as Ralph William Gosper, Jr. of Lisp fame calls them, *little programming languages*. A data structure provides the means for the organization, and storage of the data. Like other programming languages, F# comes with several built-in data structures and the capability to build new and custom abstract data types. The built-in data types in F# include the fundamental .NET types such as `integer`, `unsigned integer`, `decimal`, `short`, `long`, `unsigned short`, `unsigned long`, `byte`, `signed byte`, `bool`, `double`, `float`, `native int`, `unsigned native int`, `char`, and `string`. The details can be seen in the following table figure which describes the .NET data types and examples of their corresponding F# declarations:

.NET Data Type	F# Declaration
Int	`let i = 0 or` `let i = 0l`
Uint	`let i = 1u or` `let i = 1ul`
Decimal	`let d = 1m or` `let d = 1M`
Short	`let c = 2s`
Long	`let l = 5L`
unsigned short	`let c = 6us`
unsigned long	`let d = 7UL`

byte	`let by = 86y`
	`let by = 0b00000101y`
	`let by = 'a'B`

signed byte	`let sby = 86uy` `let sby = 0b00000101uy`
bool	`let b = true`

double	`let d = 0.2 or`
	`let d = 2e-1 or`
	`let d = 2.`
	`let d0 =`
	`0x0000000000000000LF`

float	`let f = 0.3f or`
	`let f = 0.3F or`
	`let f = 2.f`
	`let f0 =`
	`0x0000000000000001f`

native int	`let n = 4n`
unsigned native int	`let n = 4un`
char	`let c = 'a'`
string	`let str = "packt` `publishing"`
big int	`let i = 9I`

Beside these fundamental types, F# also provides a variety of advanced built-in data structures including lists, sequences, tuples, records, option types, and unions. In this chapter, we will discuss these types in greater detail and then discuss their implementation using some basic sorting algorithms.

Arrays

Arrays are among the simplest of data structures, a homogenous mutable collection of items. We saw some of the basics in *Chapter 1, Embrace the Truth*; let's review it with some of the advanced features. A basic array can be declared as follows:

```
let Philosophers = [| "Aquinas" ; "Alfarabi"; "Avicenna"; "Averroes";
"Maimonides"|];;
```

The declaration starts with let binding, `[|`; individual elements are separated by a semi-colon and it ends with `|]`.

```
val Philosophers : string [] =
    [|"Aquinas"; "Alfarabi"; "Avicenna"; "Averroes"; "Maimonides"|]
```

The individual elements of an array can be accessed with a `.[index]` suffix given as follows:

```
> Philosphers.[2]
;;
val it : string = "Avicenna"
```

If you are familiar with the C family of languages, this syntax is a bit different. If you don't use `.` before the array index, you will get the following error:

```
> Philosophers[0]
;;
  Philosophers[0]
  ^^^^^^^^^^^^


stdin(5,1): error FS0003: This value is not a function and cannot be
applied
```

The type of an array can be explicitly defined as follows:

```
let PhilosophersTyped : string [] =
    [| "Aquinas" ; "Alfarabi"; "Avicenna"; "Averroes"; "Maimonides"|]
```

You can generate long sequences of numbers within arrays using the array range syntax as a part of the array declaration.

```
let CountTo100 = [|1..100|]
```

The resulting output is as follows:

```
val CountTo100 : int [] =
  [|1; 2; 3; 4; 5; 6; 7; 8; 9; 10; 11; 12; 13; 14; 15; 16; 17; 18; 19;
20; 21;
    22; 23; 24; 25; 26; 27; 28; 29; 30; 31; 32; 33; 34; 35; 36; 37; 38;
39; 40;
    41; 42; 43; 44; 45; 46; 47; 48; 49; 50; 51; 52; 53; 54; 55; 56; 57;
58; 59;
    60; 61; 62; 63; 64; 65; 66; 67; 68; 69; 70; 71; 72; 73; 74; 75; 76;
77; 78;
    79; 80; 81; 82; 83; 84; 85; 86; 87; 88; 89; 90; 91; 92; 93; 94; 95;
96; 97;
    98; 99; 100|]
```

An advanced number sequence can be generated using the step value in the array range syntax, where the pattern is defined as follows:

```
let CountTo1000By100 = [|1..100..1000|]
```

This results in the following output:

```
val CountTo1000By100 : int [] =
  [|1; 101; 201; 301; 401; 501; 601; 701; 801; 901|]
```

The middle value defines the step and therefore can be used to perform operations like countdowns. Refer to the following line of code as an example:

```
let ReverseCount100 = [|100..-1..1|]
```

The preceding line of code generates the following result:

```
val ReverseCount100 : int [] =
  [|100; 99; 98; 97; 96; 95; 94; 93; 92; 91; 90; 89; 88; 87; 86; 85; 84;
83;
    82; 81; 80; 79; 78; 77; 76; 75; 74; 73; 72; 71; 70; 69; 68; 67; 66;
65; 64;
    63; 62; 61; 60; 59; 58; 57; 56; 55; 54; 53; 52; 51; 50; 49; 48; 47;
46; 45;
    44; 43; 42; 41; 40; 39; 38; 37; 36; 35; 34; 33; 32; 31; 30; 29; 28;
27; 26;
    25; 24; 23; 22; 21; 20; 19; 18; 17; 16; 15; 14; 13; 12; 11; 10; 9; 8;
7; 6;
    5; 4; 3; 2; 1|]
```

The Array construct in F# is pretty powerful. `Array.zeroCreate` allows you to create pre-populated arrays with zeroes or nulls.

```
// Signature:
Array.zeroCreate : int -> 'T []

// Usage:
Array.zeroCreate count
```

Here, `count` is the length of the array to be created. By default, the array will be populated with `0` in case of numeric types, and with null in case of reference types.

For numeric and all other types respectively, `Array.create` takes a number of elements and their default values as input, and creates an array with the specified default value:

```
// Signature:
Array.create : int -> 'T -> 'T []

// Usage:
Array.create count value
```

Here, `count` is the length of the array to be created, and value is the value of elements. For example, an almost ideal cricket over for a batsman would be as follows:

```
let SixSixers = Array.create 6 6
```

The preceding line of code translates to the following array:

val SixSixers : int [] = [|6; 6; 6; 6; 6; 6|]

Notice the decimal increment here using the array range syntax, in the following code snippet:

```
let zeroToSixty = [| 0.0 .. 4.5 .. 60.0 |]
```

The preceding line of code provides with following output:

val zeroToSixty : float [] =
** [|0.0; 4.5; 9.0; 13.5; 18.0; 22.5; 27.0; 31.5; 36.0; 40.5; 45.0; 49.5; 54.0;**
**   58.5|]**

`Array.init` is another handy way of initializing the array. The formal signature of the method is described as follows:

```
Array.init : int -> (int -> 'T) -> 'T []
that is, Array.init count initializer
```

For example, refer to the following line of code:

```
let ArrayofCubes = (Array.init 10 (fun index -> index * index *
index))
```

The preceding line of code results in the following array:

val ArrayofCubes : int [] = [|0; 1; 8; 27; 64; 125; 216; 343; 512; 729|]

An array can be declared in various ways. For instance, the following are a few ways of creating some stately arrays:

```
let Senators : string[] = Array.zeroCreate 100;;
let HouseReps : string array = Array.zeroCreate 435;;
let OriginalColonies = Array.zeroCreate<string> 13;;
```

Like initialization, you can also access the array elements using user-defined sequences, also known as slice notation. For instance, the following is the array declaration of IMDB's top 10 movies (aren't you glad `Citizen Kane` isn't one of them!):

```
let imdbtop10 : string[] = [|"The Shawshank Redemption (1994)";
  "The Godfather (1972)";
  "The Godfather: Part II (1974)";
  "Il buono, il brutto, il cattivo. (1966)";
  "Pulp Fiction (1994)";
  "Inception (2010)";
  "Schindler's List (1993)";
  "12 Angry Men (1957)";
  "One Flew Over the Cuckoo's Nest (1975)";
  "The Dark Knight (2008)"
|]
```

Now, if you try to retrieve these elements, you can do it in various ways, such as :

```
let TopThree = imdbtop10.[1..3];;
let TopFive = imdbtop10.[..5];;
let BottomFive = imdbtop10.[5..];;
let list = imdbtop10.[0..];;
```

This way of creation and retrieval makes it very easy for developers to manipulate arrays. You can also create multi-dimensional arrays like the following line of code:

```
let wolfenstein3d = Array3D.zeroCreate<float> 11 11 11;;
```

The assignment of the multi-dimensional array to an element goes as follows:

```
wolfenstein3d.[0,0,0] <- 1.1;;
```

The Array module in the `Microsoft.FSharp.Collections` namespace provides a wide variety of functions. If you are familiar with the .NET Framework's Base Class Library, the `namespace` keyword is used to declare a scope that contains a set of related objects. In easier terms, it is like a collection of related functionality, usually as part of a smaller assembly or a `.dll` file. It is not possible to cover them in this limited space but I would recommend exploring it further on MSDN at `http://msdn.microsoft.com/en-us/library/ee370273.aspx`.

Lists

Like arrays, a **list** in F# is a data structure which represents an immutable series of homogenous type elements, in order.

The list in F# is implemented as a singly linked list which provides linear time for element access, instant access to the list's first element. F# provides a list module with wide-ranging functions for operating on lists. The F# list is immutable and hence this collection is preferred over the .NET list collection for functional implementation. A list of numbers is declared as follows:

```
let numbers = [0; 1; 2; 3; 4; 5; 6; 7; 8; 9]
```

The preceding line of code appears in the FSI as follows:

val numbers : int list = [0; 1; 2; 3; 4; 5; 6; 7; 8; 9]

There is an important distinction to remember here. Look at the following example:

```
let numbers = [0; 1; 2; 3; 4; 5; 6; 7; 8; 9]
```

If you have used , instead of ; , the preceding statement would create a list typed to store 10-element tuples with all items being `int`, with just one element.

```
val numbers : (int * int * int * int * int * int * int * int * int *
int) list = [(0, 1, 2, 3, 4, 5, 6, 7, 8, 9)]
```

 The fundamental difference between an array and list is that arrays are a collection with a fixed size, while lists grow dynamically. Since lists are immutable, a new list is created every time a list gets modified which might lead to performance issues.

Moreover, arrays have mutable elements while a `List` contains immutable elements; also instead of using index operations to read the elements like arrays, Lists use recursion and pattern matching for this purpose. Most of the array functions are similar in a `List` collection as well. The following is an example of how a list is created, and later an element is concatenated to it using the `::` cons operator. In the third line, you can see a string being extracted using an array index, and further indexing into the extracted string to get a substring. In the fourth line, you also see the concatenation of lists using the `@` operator:

```
let yodaQuotesFragment1 = [" Must ";" Unlearn ";" What ";" You "]

let yodaQuotesFragment2 = "You "::yodaQuotesFragment1

let yodaQuotesFragment3 = [yodaQuotesFragment1.[1].[3..7] + "ed"]

let yodaQuote = yodaQuotesFragment2 @ yodaQuotesFragment3
```

The preceding code snippet will result an output as follows:

```
val yodaQuotesFragment1 : string list =
  [" Must "; " Unlearn "; " What "; " You "]
val yodaQuotesFragment2 : string list =
  ["You "; " Must "; " Unlearn "; " What "; " You "]
val yodaQuotesFragment3 : string list = ["learned"]
val yodaQuote : string list =
  ["You "; " Must "; " Unlearn "; " What "; " You "; "learned"]
```

Some of the list type operations can be seen in the following table:

List Operation	Output
`yodaQuote.IsEmpty;;`	`val it : bool = false`
`yodaQuote.Length;;`	`val it : bool = false`
`yodaQuote.Head;;`	`val it : int = 6` `val it : string = "You "`
`yodaQuote.Tail;;`	`val it : string list = [" Must "; " Unlearn "; " What "; " You "; "learned"]`
`yodaQuote.Item (1);;`	`val it : string = " Must"`

Due to their immutability, linear access, and cons operation, lists are highly suitable for recursive operations. The `List` module also provides sort, search, and arithmetic operations on lists.

Lists allow for zip and unzip operations. Wondering why there's no tar and gzip support yet? This is not related to compression. The zip operation takes two collections and combines them into tuples as follows:

```
let FirstNames = ["Walter "; "Skyler"; "Jesse"; "Hank"; "Saul" ]
let LastNames = ["White "; "White"; "Pinkman"; "Schrader"; "Goodman" ]

let BreakingBadCast = List.zip FirstNames LastNames
```

```
val BreakingBadCast : (string * string) list =
  [("Walter ", "White "); ("Skyler", "White"); ("Jesse", "Pinkman");
  ("Hank", "Schrader"); ("Saul", "Goodman")]
```

A list can be iterated as follows:

```
>List.iter (fun x -> printfn "%s" x) FirstNames
>
Walter
Skyler
Jesse
Hank
Saul
val it : unit = ()
>
```

 The filter, map, and fold operations of List provide significant benefits in writing functional, idiomatic code. We will discuss these in details in upcoming chapters.

List comprehensions

List comprehension is a fancy word for the kind of syntactic sugar you have seen earlier in the case of arrays, the slicing and ranges. Several languages provide these capabilities to a list so they can populate the data structures using intelligent predicates. As seen in the case of arrays in the *Arrays* section of this chapter, list comprehensions are the syntactic sugar provided to generate lists. In F#, ranges and generators provide syntactic sugar which allows us to perform operations like the following code snippet:

```
> [-100..0];;
```

```
> [1..10..100];;
```

```
> ['A'..'Z'];;
```

The output for the preceding operations operations is as follows:

```
val it : int list =
  [-100; -99; -98; -97; -96; -95; -94; -93; -92; -91; -90; -89; -88; -87;
-86;   -85; -84; -83; -82; -81; -80; -79; -78; -77; -76; -75; -74; -73;
-72; -71;   -70; -69; -68; -67; -66; -65; -64; -63; -62; -61; -60; -59;
-58; -57; -56;   -55; -54; -53; -52; -51; -50; -49; -48; -47; -46; -45;
-44; -43; -42; -41;   -40; -39; -38; -37; -36; -35; -34; -33; -32; -31;
-30; -29; -28; -27; -26;   -25; -24; -23; -22; -21; -20; -19; -18; -17;
-16; -15; -14; -13; -12; -11;   -10; -9; -8; -7; -6; -5; -4; -3; -2; -1;
...]
>
val it : int list = [1; 11; 21; 31; 41; 51; 61; 71; 81; 91]
> val it : char list =
  ['A'; 'B'; 'C'; 'D'; 'E'; 'F'; 'G'; 'H'; 'I'; 'J'; 'K'; 'L'; 'M'; 'N';
'O';
  'P'; 'Q'; 'R'; 'S'; 'T'; 'U'; 'V'; 'W'; 'X'; 'Y'; 'Z']
```

Generators are a more flexible construct with the following syntax:

```
for x in collection do ... yield expr
```

Revisiting the earlier `cube` function, a simple list can be defined as follows:

```
[ for x in 1 .. 10 do
  yield (x * x * x) ];;
```

The preceding syntax generates the list of cubes of numbers from 1 to 10:

```
val it : int list = [1; 8; 27; 64; 125; 216; 343; 512; 729; 1000]
```

Sequences

An easy way to distinguish sequences from the rest of the data structures which we discussed earlier is to call them Schrödinger's lists (Schrödinger's cat); that is, a data structure which contains elements which are evaluated on demand. It is important to note here that `seq<'a>` is an alias, or a type abbreviation for `IEnumerable<'a>`, and is compatible with any .NET type implementing `IEnumerable`, including lists, arrays, sets, and maps. Like arrays and lists, sequences contain homogenous data elements but the elements are computed lazily or on an as needed basis.

The syntax for defining a sequence is quite straightforward:

```
let countToTen = seq { 1..10 }
```

The result in FSI is as follows:

```
val countToTen : seq<int>
```

The sequence only gets populated when we request it:

```
> countToTen
;;
val it : seq<int> = seq [1; 2; 3; 4; ...]
>
```

The following construct will return the corresponding length when inquired, that is, computed on-demand, and only gets populated when requested:

```
let countToTenLength = countToTen |> Seq.length
```

Using similar comprehensions, we can find out the existence of elements in a sequence as a function as follows:

```
let alphabets = seq { 'a'..'z' }

alphabets |> Seq.exists (fun c -> c = 'x')
```

The preceding code segment returns true since character x exists in the sequence, which is computed when it searches for the character:

```
val alphabets : seq<char>

val it : bool = true
```

As a word of warning, it is not always a good idea to ask for deterministic aggregate functions (like length) on an infinite-style data structure such as sequence. A good example of lazy evaluation can be looking at our national debt:

```
let nationalDebt = seq { 1I .. 18000000000000I };;
```

Now, contrary to how an array or a list would interpret this, the sequence does not evaluate or populate the 18 trillion dollars here. We can now proceed and create another list using nationalDebt as follows:

```
let myShare = Seq.truncate 186233 nationalDebt
```

This new sequence is created by truncating the existing one. Now, I can convert this truncated sequence into a list and evaluate its length, which as you guessed will be equal to my share of national debt:

```
myShare |> Seq.toList |> List.length
```

However, doing the following is definitely not a good idea:

```
nationalDebt |> Seq.length
```

Sequences are powerful structures, and with great power comes great responsibility.

Tuples and records

Unlike the data structures studied above, **tuples** (pronounced two-pull, instead of rhyming with couple, unless of course you speak British English) represent a collection which allows the storage of heterogeneous types. Refer to the following line of code for an example of a tuple:

```
let hodgepodge = ("xkcd", 3.142, System.Math.PI, 0xFFFFFF,"the
oatmeal");;
```

The FSI output of the preceding statement shows the automatic type inference as follows:

```
val hodgepodge : string * float * float * int * string =

  ("xkcd", 3.142, 3.141592654, 16777215, "the oatmeal")
```

Tuples are highly useful as function parameters and return types. A few examples follow:

```
let morehodgepodge = (System.Math.PI * System.Math.E, "Path not found.
Try the grass shortcut",("Hello","World"), printfn "I come first!");;
```

```
>
```

```
I come first!
```

```
val morehodgepodge : float * string * (string * string) * unit =

  (8.539734223, "Path not found.  Try the grass shortcut", ("Hello",
"World"),

  null)
```

```
let circumference (x:float, y:float, z:float) = (2.0 * System.Math.PI
* x, 2.0 * System.Math.PI * y, 2.0 * System.Math.PI * z);;
```

```
> circumference (10.0, 20.0, 35.0);;
```

```
val it : float * float * float = (62.83185307, 125.6637061, 219.9114858)
```

A record is a named field tuple.

```
type recordName =    { [ fieldName : dataType ] + }}
```

The preceding line of code can also be represented as following for clarity in a less terse form:

```
type recordName = {
  [ mutable ] fieldName1 : dataType1;
  [ mutable ] fieldName2 : dataType2;
  ...
  }
```

For example:

```
type MacOSRelease =
  { Title: string;
    Version : string }
```

Once a type is defined, the F# compiler is intelligent enough to deduce what type a particular record belongs to, for instance:

```
let beta = {Title="Kodiak"; Version="Beta"};;
let v10_0 = {Title="Cheetah"; Version="10.0"};;
let V10_1  = {Title="Puma"; Version="10.1"};;
let v10_2 = {Title="Jaguar"; Version="10.2"};;
let v10_3 = {Title="Panther"; Version="10.3"};;
let v10_4 = {Title="Tiger"; Version="10.4"};;
let v10_5 = {Title="Leopard"; Version="10.5"};;
let v10_6 = {Title="Snow Leopard"; Version="10.6"};;
let v10_7 = {Title="Lion"; Version="10.7"};;
let v10_8 = {Title="Mountain Lion"; Version="10.8"};;
let v10_9 = {Title="Mavericks"; Version="10.9"};;
let v10_10 = {Title="Yosemite"; Version="10.10"};;
```

In the first line of the preceding code, `beta` is recognized as follows:

```
val beta : MacOSRelease = {Title = "Kodiak";
   Version = "Beta";}
```

Option types

Option types, also known as `Some()` and `None()`, represent simplistic data structures which can hold two possible values. They are used when a real value may not exist to depict whether a computation was successful or failed. Option type is typically used in pattern matching for its friendly syntax. If a function exists, it returns `true` if the option has a value, and will return `false` if it does not. You will see the extensive use of option types in future chapters, but take a look at the following code for example:

```
let isEven (n : int) = if n % 2 = 0 then Some(n) else None
```

```
> isEven 3;;
val it : int option = None
```

and

```
> isEven 4;;
val it : int option = Some 4
```

Sets and maps

The Set data structure in F# is similar to collections discussed earlier such as lists. However, it does not allow for duplicates and does not preserve their order. It also allows for typical set operations such as IsProperSubsetOf, IsProperSupersetOf, IsSubsetOf, IsSupersetOf, and specialized operations such as MaximumElement and MinimumElement. The collection also provides union and subtraction operations.

A Set can be defined as follows:

```
let androidVersions = Set.empty.Add("Cupcake").Add("Donut").
Add("Eclair").Add("Froyo").Add("Gingerbread").Add("Honeycomb").
Add("Ice Cream Sandwich").Add("Jelly Bean").Add("KitKat")
```

The additions can be performed later on, as shown in the following line of code:

```
androidVersions.Add ("Lollipop")
```

Since sets are immutable, the add operation produces a new set and does not mutate the original set. As the underlying binary tree implementation, the new set will share many storage nodes with the original.

Utility functions like Set.ofList, Set.ofArray, and Set.ofSeq can be used to convert different collections into sets, provided there are no duplicates. If duplicate elements are found, they are simply removed.

Maps, like records in tuples allow key-value pair association for effective use of the collection. Maps add key-value pair associations so that you can use map collections as dictionaries. See the following code (due to formatting changes, the following code must be rearranged to run within the FSI):

```
let bibTeXBiblio = Map.empty.
Add("agrawal1996fast", "Fast Discovery of Association Rules.")
.Add("bell2009beyond", "Beyond the data deluge")
.Add("Wooldridge2003", "Bayesian Belief Networks")
.Add("Witten2005", "Data Mining: Practical machine learning tools and
techniques");;

bibTeXBiblio.["Wooldridge2003"]

val it : string = "Bayesian Belief Networks"
```

Discriminated unions

Remember the option type (Some, None) that we discussed in the previous section? It is a specialized case of a discriminated union with two union cases, either something or nothing. Discriminated union is a union type to define named cases, similar to how the Union type is defined in various other languages. For example, in C, it enables us to store different data types in the same memory location. The F# language specification defines the syntax of discriminated unions as follows:

```
type type-name =
    | case-identifier1 [of [ fieldname1 : ] type1 [ * [ fieldname2 : ]
type2 ...]
    | case-identifier2 [of [fieldname3 : ]type3 [ * [ fieldname4 : ]
type4 ...]
    ...
```

Discriminated union depicts a well-defined named set of available cases. This type is used to build complex data structures, and recursive discriminated unions are used to represent trees. The difference between a record type and discriminated unions is that of and and or. A record represents a tuple with labels, while the discriminated union can be seen as a union of different types.

An example of single type discriminated union follows:

```
type Title = string
type Rating = string
type Plot = string
type Ranking = float
type Year = int

type Movie = Movie of Title * Rating * Plot * Ranking * Year

let Serenity = Movie("Serenity", "PG-13", "The crew of the ship
Serenity tries to evade an assassin sent to recapture one of their
number who is telepathic.", 8.0, 2005)
```

There are cases when you would want to mix types; for instance build a hybrid type where an instance can be either bool, or string, but not both. Such types are ubiquitous in real world programming scenarios when data elements are multi-natured. The following is an example with discriminated union:

```
type Human = {first:string; last:string}

type IntelligentBeing =
    | Robot of float * int //model and year
```

```
      | H of Human

   let unit1  = Robot (8.5, 2051)
   let unit2  = H {first="Stephen"; last="Hawking"}
```

The preceding code results in the following:

```
type Human =
  {first: string;
    last: string;}


type IntelligentBeing =
  | Robot of float * int
  | H of Human


val unit1 : IntelligentBeing = Robot (8.5,2051)

val unit2 : IntelligentBeing = H {first = "Stephen";
  last = "Hawking";}
```

The active pattern

Now that you have gained some basic familiarity with discriminated unions, it will be rather easy now to explain active patterns, the named partitions to split up the input data. The F# language specification defines an active pattern as follows:

```
// Complete active pattern definition.
let (|identifer1|identifier2|...|) [ arguments ] = expression
// Partial active pattern definition.
let (|identifier|_|) [ arguments ] = expression
```

A simple use case for an active pattern can be something as basic as an even/odd classifier:

```
let (|Even|Odd|) x = if x % 2 <> 0 then Odd else Even
```

Upon execution with even and odd numbers, the results are either choice 1 or choice 2:

```
>(|Even|Odd|) 5;;
val it : Choice<unit,unit> = Choice2Of2 null
```

A more practical use case can be getting an instance of a particular service bus object as shown in the following code. The snippet is incomplete and expects some pre-requisite objects to be created and is shown to demonstrate a potential real-world scenario:

```
let (|ToServiceObject|) x =
    match x with
    | "NServiceBus"   -> NServiceBus.Instance
    | "MuleESB"  -> MuleESB.Instance
    | "RabbitMQ" -> RabbitMQ.Instance
    | _          -> failwith "Unknown Object"

let (ToServiceObject object) = "RabbitMQ"
```

F# implementation of sorting algorithms

In this section, we will review a few common sorting algorithms, and their functional style implementation in F#. Quick sort, bubble sort, and merge sort are fairly easy to understand sorting algorithms and are commonly taught in the introduction to algorithm courses. The purpose of using them here, is to reinforce the idea of functional constructs discussed earlier, and show their usage in a practical setting.

Algorithmic complexity and the Big-O notation

Big-O notation provides a relative measure for complexity of an algorithm. In contrast with the *theta* (two-sided bound), Big-O is the upper bound of the complexity which, in layman terms, shows what would be the worst case scenario complexity based on the number of operations it would take.

The complexity of an algorithm is an important concept for developers to understand; if a problem can be addressed in a single pass, and your solution somehow addresses it in a nested loop, you have dramatically increased the number of operations, hence making your approach ultimately unusable for large scale problems.

There are various different classes of problems based on their algorithmic complexity; the lowest value is better. Easily solved problems include those which can be solved in constant $O(1)$, logarithmic $O(\log n)$ linear $O(n)$, linear-logarithmic $O(n \log n)$, quadratic $O(n^2)$, or cubic form $O(n^3)$. The exponential $O(2^n)$ and factorial $O(n!)$ based problems are hard to solve given the time-space restrictions. How these complexities potentially impact the time-space tradeoff (based on the number of operations), can be seen in the following graph:

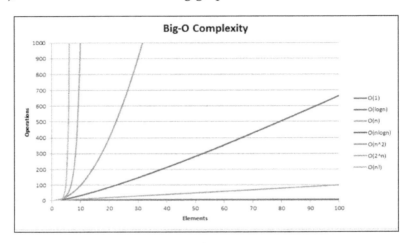

The complexity of various sorting algorithms can be seen in the following table:

Sorting Algorithm	Best Case	Average Case	Worst Case
Quick sort	$n \log n$	$n \log n$	n^2
Merge sort	$n \log n$	$n \log n$	$n \log n$
Heap sort	$n \log n$	$n \log n$	$n \log n$
Bubble sort	n	n^2	n^2
Selection sort	n^2	n^2	n^2

The bubble sort

Bubble sort is one of the simplest sorting algorithms which is easy to understand and to visualize. It is probably the most intuitive algorithm one could come up with, without thinking much. However, due to its n^2 complexity, it is practically unusable for larger datasets since it will take too long.

The Bubble sort algorithm is to iterate over the list and perform comparisons. If element *n* is smaller than element *n+1*, do the swap. These swaps will result in the larger values to be pushed upwards in the list (bubbling upwards). Once there are no swaps left to be made, the algorithm terminates. The algorithmic representation of Bubble sort can be seen as follows:

```
repeat
    hasChanged := false
    decrement itemCount
    repeat with index from 1 to itemCount
        if (item at index) > (item at (index + 1))
            swap (item at index) with (item at (index + 1))
            hasChanged := true
until hasChanged = false
```

It is fairly easy to translate the preceding algorithm into F#. First build a simple swap method which swaps the two values *x* and *y* in the array:

```
let swap x y (array : 'arr []) =
  let temp = array.[x]
  array.[x] <- array.[y]
  array.[y] <- temp
```

Now the implementation can be made very identical to the algorithm as follows:

```
let bubbleSort array =
  let rec loop (array : 'arr []) =
    let mutable swaps = 0
    for i = 0 to array.Length - 2 do
      if array.[i] > array.[i+1] then
        swap i (i+1) array
        swaps <- swaps + 1
    if swaps > 0 then loop array else array
  loop array
```

When you run this algorithm on the array of numbers as shown next, you would get a sorted array as a result:

```
> let arr = [|5; 4; 8; 20; 1|];;

val arr : int [] = [|5; 4; 8; 20; 1|]

> bubbleSort arr;;
val it : int [] = [|1; 4; 5; 8; 20|]
```

However, this algorithm implementation is not idiomatically functional, as you have probably noticed. The implementation is imperative, destructive (relies on mutability), and cycles through using loops. An improved version would allow us to use functional constructs such as recursion and lists, and utilize immutability, the head and tail operation of lists.

Like swap, this recursive method `getHighest` will get the highest value of the list:

```
let rec getHighest list =
  match list with
  | head1 :: head2 :: tail when head1 > head2 -> getHighest (head1 ::
tail)
  | head1 :: head2 :: tail -> getHighest (head2::tail)
  | head1 :: [] -> head1
  | _ -> failwith "Unrecognized pattern"
```

And the actual bubble sort implementation is a recursive method which partitions the list, applies the function to get the highest value and maintains a sorted return list in case the array hasn't been sorted:

```
let bubbleSort_func list =
  let rec innerBubbleSort sorted = function
  | [] -> sorted
  | l ->
    let h = getHighest l
    let (x, y) = List.partition (fun i -> i = h) l
    innerBubbleSort (x @ sorted) y
  innerBubbleSort [] list
```

Now, if we take an unsorted array and apply the newly minted functional method to it, the following would be the result:

```
val data : int list =
  [1683249965; 135774752; 1627998559; 1112950566; 373482178;
1031234918;
  505894459; 306487619; 1126406242; 1370137881]
```

`> bubbleSort_func data;;`

`val it : int list =`

  `[135774752; 306487619; 373482178; 505894459; 1031234918; 1112950566;`

  `1126406242; 1370137881; 1627998559; 1683249965]`

The functional implementation, due to the use of GetHighest, is now closer to Selection sort. As defined above, in pure bubble sort we compare neighboring items and swap which is done in GetHighest minus the preservation.

Quicksort

Quicksort, one of the fastest generalized sorting algorithms, was introduced by *C. A. R Hoare*, a famous British computer scientist and inventor of null reference, for which he publically apologized. Quicksort operates by performing a partition operation based on a pivot element, and then divides the array into sub-arrays. The selection of pivot can be either randomized, median based, or based on some strategy depending on the dataset. Due to its partitioning nature, Quicksort is also known as partition-exchange sort.

A Quicksort algorithm can be easily explained as follows:

```
function quicksort(array)
    less, equal, greater := three empty arrays
    if length(array) > 1
        pivot := select any element of array
        for each x in array
            if x < pivot then add x to less
            if x = pivot then add x to equal
            if x > pivot then add x to greater
        quicksort(less)
        quicksort(greater)
        array := concatenate(less, equal, greater)
```

As the preceding algorithm describes, Quicksort partitions the array and performs the majority of work splitting and sorting and using recursive calls there. The join afterwards is a fairly trivial task. A functional implementation of Quicksort, as we have seen in *Chapter 2, Now Lazily Get Over It, Again*, is given as follows:

```
let rec quickSort = function
    | [] -> []
    | n::ns -> let lessthan, greaterEqual = List.partition ((>) n) ns
        quickSort lessthan @ n :: quickSort greaterEqual
```

The implementation translates the algorithm quite well. Applying this operation on the `10000` randomized numbers as follows:

```
let rand = new System.Random()
let data = List.init 10000 (fun _  -> rand.Next())
let result = quickSort data
```

Results show fairly quick performance as can be seen via the `#time` directive:

```
Real: 00:00:00.218, CPU: 00:00:00.280, GC gen0: 2, gen1: 1, gen2: 1
```

```
val result : int list =
  [497219; 841552; 938558; 1071943; 1084497; 1520120; 1906074; 2320008;
    2548170; 2643728; 2951999; 3065102; 3211945; 3633292; 3650083;
3805526;
    3834393; 3843040; 4247641; 4338248; 4415092; 5341969; 5489570;
5831599;
    6004183; 6309715; 6338136; 6727287; 7633883; 8104068; 8126910;
8157719;
    20390950; 20731085; 20813950; 20824286; 20840531; 21357667; 21588276;
    21779370; 21923241; 22250333; 23053679; ...]
```

However, it should be realized that built-in algorithms are still very fast. For instance, the same `List.Sort` method will operate at a much faster pace:

```
#time
let result2 = List.sort data
#time
```

The built-in operation will operate in 5 milliseconds as compared to 218 milliseconds:

```
Real: 00:00:00.005, CPU: 00:00:00.000, GC gen0: 0, gen1: 0, gen2: 0
```

So re-invent the wheel of your new data structures with care!

The merge sort

Merge sort is a divide and conquer recursive sort with the best, worst, and average case of $n \log n$. It operates by dividing the input array into smaller groups of one and then merge (hence the name, merge sort) these elements in order.

The algorithm for the merge sort is outlined as follows:

```
function mergesort(m)
    var list left, right, result
    if length(m) ≤ 1
        return m
    else
        var middle = length(m) / 2
        for each x in m up to middle - 1
            add x to left
        for each x in m at and after middle
            add x to right
        left = mergesort(left)
        right = mergesort(right)
        if last(left) ≤ first(right)
            append right to left
            return left
        result = merge(left, right)
        return result

function merge(left,right)
    var list result
    while length(left) > 0 and length(right) > 0
        if first(left) ≤ first(right)
            append first(left) to result
            left = rest(left)
        else
            append first(right) to result
            right = rest(right)
    if length(left) > 0
        append rest(left) to result
    if length(right) > 0
        append rest(right) to result
    return result
```

There are essentially two segments of the merge sort—split and join. The splitting of the list with the accumulator pattern can be accomplished as follows:

```
let split list =
  let rec aux l acc1 acc2 =
    match l with
      | [] -> (acc1,acc2)
      | [x] -> (x::acc1,acc2)
      | x::y::tail ->
        aux tail (x::acc1) (y::acc2)
  in aux list [] []
```

Accumulator is the variable used to build the result of a computation. Functionally speaking, an accumulator underpins the fold construct. For instance, in a function which finds the product of the elements of a list, the accumulator holds the cumulative product while the algorithm gets executed.

Similarly, the merge operation of the lists can be accomplished recursively as follows:

```
let rec merge l1 l2 =
  match (l1,l2) with
    | (x,[]) -> x
    | ([],y) -> y
    | (x::tx,y::ty) ->
      if x <= y then x::merge tx l2
      else y::merge l1 ty
```

Combining the merge and split operations together, the implementation becomes the recursive split of the lists as follows:

```
let rec mergesort list =
  match list with
    | [] -> []
    | [x] -> [x]
    | _ -> let (l1,l2) = split list
      in merge (mergesort l1) (mergesort l2)
```

Running the program with `10000` records can be easily accomplished as follows:

```
let data = List.init 10000 (fun _  -> rand.Next())
#time
let result = mergesort data
#time
```

As expected, the time taken here is significantly higher than the quick sort implementation:

```
Real: 00:00:00.160, CPU: 00:00:00.156, GC gen0: 1, gen1: 0, gen2: 0


val result : int list =
  [374356; 766306; 856446; 985913; 1069646; 1091214; 1100056; 1186442;
1220909;   1455576; 1823274; 1852283; 2155459; 2156636; 2217031; 2315991;
2495221;   2803701; 3145611; 3257821; 3537969; 3899291; 3996007; 4376478;
4567141;   5212057; 5218364; 5277498; 5932082; 6566236; 6577270; 7004511;
7129935;   7301935; 8105732; 8552139; 8575302; 8839833; 9164862; 9204331;
9314072;   9369207; 9392614; 9663778; 9779735; 9858032; 10415031;
10645283; 11106144;
```

```
   11233419; 11342086; 11357700; 11527141; 11680468; 11809579; 11923824;
11932616; 12035918; 12050695; 12080661; 12090218; 12172926; 12190249;
12609284; 12622441; 13233787; 13888352; 14395337; 14486154; 14498550;
14947146; 15023921; 15570504; 16017556; 16148514; 16223650; 16727490;
17036182; 17106224; 17147584; 17157593; 17248072; 17319881; 17560458;
17578398; 18175603; 18510321; 18547633; 18606260; 18624345; 18670559;
18801345; 19134084; 19357011; 19595348; 19864199; 20050435; 20319318;
20435156; 20641522; ...]
```

```
--> Timing now off
```

In this chapter, we have presented several sorting algorithms and their implementation in F#. The goal of this chapter was not an in-depth discussion of these algorithms but rather to get the reader familiar with the functional and idiomatic ways of implementing them. As seen in the bubble sort example, the traditional way of implementing an algorithm can easily be improved upon to use functional constructs.

 For further in-depth reading of the big-O notation, cyclomatic complexity, sorting and related algorithms, we would recommend reading *Pearls of Functional Algorithm Design* by Richard Bird, *Introduction to Algorithms* by Cormen et al (the CLRS book), and *Algorithm Design Manual* by Steven Skiena.

Summary

In this chapter, we covered the built-in data structures along with distinguishing between the mutable (stateful) and immutable ones. We presented common operations on array, list, set, and map. We provided an introduction to list comprehensions, active pattern, querying (for example, groupBy), along with an overview of sorting algorithms. We also included a discussion of the Big-O notation and how it impacts the runtime of different algorithms.

In the next chapter, we will gain further knowledge about enumerations and sequences. We will delve into sequence expression (seq), implementation of custom enumeration for the purpose of sequence expression (that is, paging functionality), and the application of simple custom types using records and tuples. You will see filtering and enumerating a sequence, from a simple CSV file and implementing custom enumerator for paging purposes.

4

Are We There Yet?

"More computing sins are committed in the name of efficiency (without necessarily achieving it) than for any other single reason."

– William A. Wulf

Most good programmers do programming not because they expect to get paid or get adulation by the public, but because it is fun to program."

– Linus Torvalds

This chapter provides a detailed primer to one of the fundamental functional data structures in F#, that is, **sequences**. Functional programming and idiomatic expressions are amazing but, until you understand the fundamental constructs and how they work together, you cannot create meaningful expressions. One of the challenges that beginners find while learning functional programming is the trend to promote features instead of solving problems and explaining fundamentals. Some features are promoted to be so clever that the authors stop thinking about the problem and start focusing on the clever features; it is actually quite hard to resist.

We will explore the **enumerations** and **sequence** expressions (seq) in detail, and will explore the implementation of custom enumeration for the purpose of sequence expression, that is, paging functionality. Functional programming has so many excellent concepts that you stop thinking about the problem you are trying to solve and start exploring combinators, monads, and so on. In this chapter, we focus on the practical aspects of what you have learned so far, and implement these constructs.

You will learn to perform various operations on sequences including filtering and enumerating a sequence. Last, but not least, we will review the pros and cons of using sequences in real-world applications and related concerns.

In this chapter, we will cover the following topics:

- Enumerations and sequences
- Typical operations on sequences
- Implementing custom enumerations (paging)
- Filtering and enumerating a sequence
- Query expressions

Diving deep into enumerations and sequences

You may recall that we discussed enumerations and sequences in *Chapter 3, What's in the Bag Anyway,* where we explain sequences as Schrödinger's lists, that is, a data structure that contains elements that are evaluated on demand. Under the covers, the sequence `seq<'T>` or `'T seq` is just `IEnumerable<'T>` for a generic type `T`, which is now a commonly used construct since the introduction of LINQ to the .NET Framework. It won't be incorrect to say that introducing LINQ to .NET was the beginning of functionalization of C#. Many functional features you see in C# nowadays are borrowed from, or have been cross-pollinated during, F# development and subsequent integration with CLR.

In the .NET framework class library, `IEnumerable<'T>` is defined as an interface that exposes an enumerator to iterate over a collection. An interface provides a relationship to the type, and is basically a collection of attributes and methods. It serves as a contract, and the actual implementation of an interface is provided in the class that implements it.

As an interface, `IEnumerable<'T>` defines the behavior while the F# sequence implements it. As defined earlier, it is important to note here that `seq<'T>` is an alias, or a type abbreviation for `IEnumerable<'T>`, and is compatible with any .NET type implementing `IEnumerable`, including `list`, `array`, `sets`, and `maps`. Sequence is a list of potential values to be evaluated and computed on demand. As seen earlier, we create new sequences using sequence expressions. The syntax for defining a sequence with the range expression is quite straightforward:

```
let countToTen = seq { 1..10 }
```

The results in FSI show that a sequence of int has been created:

```
val countToTen : seq<int>
```

It is important to notice that evaluation is lazy by default; this sequence only gets populated when we request it:

```
> countToTen
;;
val it : seq<int> = seq [1; 2; 3; 4; ...]
>
```

Like arrays, sequences are also homogenous collections, that is, elements in a sequence are of the same type. Sequences are immutable; however, the elements inside are not necessarily so. You can have a sequence of some mutable class instances that will allow you to change a particular object within the collection. F# provides a rich functional syntax and library for creating and processing sequences. One of the great examples is the seq expression.

Beside the range expression, a sequence expression can also be used to create a sequence. This expression comprises of seq followed by the sequence definition. Following are some examples for creating sequences using seq:

Creating a sequence from 1-10 using the sequence expression:

```
seq { 0..10 };;
val it : seq<int> = seq [0; 1; 2; 3; ...]
```

Creating a sequence from 0.0 – 10.0, this time using the floating type:

```
seq { 0.0..10.0 }
val it : seq<float> = seq [0.0; 1.0; 2.0; 3.0; ...]
```

Sequence comprehensions are intelligent and also know their a, b, c's. Here, we are creating a sequence from a-z:

```
seq { 'a'..'z' }
val it : seq<char> = seq ['a'; 'b'; 'c'; 'd'; ...]
```

A simple stepping instruction in the sequence comprehension will allow the sequence to skip from the initial number by n, in this case 10:

```
seq { 0..10..100 }
val it : seq<int> = seq [0; 10; 20; 30; ...]
```

A step can be negative and thus help decrement the sequence as well:

```
seq { 99..-1..0 }
val it : seq<int> = seq [99; 98; 97; 96; ...]
```

The `seq` expression can also use a code segment and a yield expression to get its values. For example:

```
let intExp =
  seq {
    for i in 0..999 do
      yield i
  }
```

`Yield` can be written in short form as an arrow:

```
let intExp =
  seq {
    for i in 0..999 -> i
  }
```

Using `yield` or `->` expresses that each iteration generates a single element of the sequence. If you would rather have each iteration produce a sequence of elements instead of a single element, use the (yield bang) `yield!` operator that returns a subsequence, merged into the final sequence as follows:

```
seq { for i in 0 .. 10 .. 100 do
  yield! seq {i .. 1 .. i+9}}
val it : seq<int> = seq [0; 1; 2; 3; ...]
```

There are various highly useful functions in the `Seq` module such as `Seq.init` and `Seq.initInfinite` to generate sequences.

The `Seq.init` module takes two parameters—first one being the length of the sequence and the second one, a generator function that is used to generate each sequence element. The generator function also takes an integer argument.

The following is an example of the `Seq.init` method:

```
let integers = Seq.init 1000 (fun i -> i + 1)
val integers : seq<int>
```

Due to lazy evaluation, the generator function doesn't actually get called until the sequence element is accessed:

```
> printfn "%A" integers;;
seq [1; 2; 3; 4; ...]
val it : unit = ()
```

The `Seq.initInfinite` method is similar to `Seq.init` minus the length argument, that is, to imply infinity and beyond:

```
let integers = Seq.initInfinite (fun i -> i + 1)
```

Here you can print the potentially infinite sequence of $\frac{1}{n^3}, \frac{1}{n^3}, \frac{1}{n^3}$, bound only by the capacity of float. Infinite sequences are quite valuable to improve readability by separating different parts of an algorithm:

```
let intsInf = Seq.initInfinite (fun i ->
  let n = float( i + 1 )
  1.0 / (n * n * n))
seq [1.0; 0.125; 0.03703703704; 0.015625; ...]
val it : unit = ()
```

Calling `Seq.length` to try to get the length of an infinite sequence will result in an `InvalidOperationException`. Sequences are suited for iterating over elements and even though they don't have the `seq.[i]` accessor, it is still possible to evaluate a particular index through `Seq.nth` and `Seq.take`. One of the methods in `Seq` module, `Seq.iter`, provides support for iteration over a sequence. You can call it as follows:

```
seq { 0..9 } |> Seq.iter (printfn "%i");;
```

```
>
0
1
2
3
4
5
6
7
8
9
val it : unit = ()
>
```

A sequence can be filtered using the `Seq.filter` function. This function takes a predicate, which follows the same concept as `Where` from LINQ or SQL. The following example presents a filter to print only odd numbers from an array:

```
let arr = [|1..1000|]

let odds =
  arr
  |> Seq.filter (fun i -> i%2 <> 0)

val odds : seq<int>

> odds
;;
val it : seq<int> = seq [1; 3; 5; 7; ...]
```

Map operations allow you to apply a function to an entire list, or to a sequence in this case. The following shows how you can apply the square operation on each element of the entire sequence:

```
seq { 0..999 } |> Seq.map (fun i -> i * i);;

val it : seq<int> = seq [0; 1; 4; 9; ...]
```

The `Seq` module also offers support for sorting a sequence via `Seq.sortBy`. You can pass through the sequence via the piping operator to the `sort` method, which returns a new sorted sequence:

```
let sequence = seq { 10 .. -1 .. 1 } |> Seq.sort;;

val it : seq<int> = seq [1; 2; 3; 4; ...]
```

As noticed, the results come after you ask to evaluate the `sequence`; this is not shown.

To fold or not to fold, this is a very functional question. The folding operation is another one of the services provided by the `Seq` module. The fold method takes the sequence as an input, a function of two arguments, and an initial value as seen in the signature below:

```
Seq.fold : ('State -> 'T -> 'State) -> 'State -> seq<'T> -> 'State
```

In the preceding signature, type: `'State -> 'T -> 'State` is the function that updates the state with each element from the sequence. The `State` represents the initial state and `seq<'T>` shows the input sequence. Folding operates on the sequence by applying the function to the sequence's first element, and then recursively folding the function for the rest of the sequence. For example, the following fold implements a sum operation:

```
seq { 1 .. 100 } |> Seq.fold (fun x y -> x + y) 0;;
```

You will notice that the folding function here takes x, the accumulator variable to keep the running total, and y, the current element, and sums them up recursively until the total is reached as seen next:

val it : int = 5050

This example demonstrates one way of performing addition using fold. The curious looking 0 at the end of the function is the initial aggregation value.

During the execution of `fold`, the aggregate function is applied to each and every element of the sequence, and a new aggregate value is returned for next use. This statement can be simplified as follows by using the addition (+) operator since it is functionally equivalent:

```
seq { 1..100 } |> Seq.fold (+) 0;;
val it : int = 5050
```

The following is another example where the `fold` operation is being applied to a smaller set of floating point elements:

```
Seq.fold (+) 0.0 [1.0; 2.0; 3.0];;
val it : float = 6.0
```

Similar to `fold`, `reduce` also applies a function to each element of the sequence, starting with applying the function to the initial two elements of the sequence:

```
seq { 1 .. 100 } |> Seq.reduce (+);;
val it : int = 5050
```

The fundamental difference between `fold` and `reduce` is that `fold` requires an explicit initial value for the accumulator. However, `reduce` uses the first element as the opening accumulator. Therefore, if an empty input list is provided, `reduce` will result in an exception.

There are easier ways to calculate the sum using the `Seq` module; how about using the `sum` function as follows?

```
seq { 1..100 } |> Seq.sum;;
```

```
val it : int = 5050
```

Another popular aggregate method is `average`, which calculates the average of the given collection as seen in the following example:

```
seq { 1.0..100.0 } |> Seq.average;;
val it : float = 50.5
```

Enumerating a CSV file

As you probably have noticed by now, a sequence is quite a versatile data structure and we can use a file to populate a sequence. As seen in the next screenshot, I have created a tab-separated text file with the information about some programming languages, and their respective designers or creators:

Like various other methods specified earlier for populating a sequence, it can also easily be seeded by reading from the text file as follows:

```
let data = seq { use s = new System.IO.StreamReader("ProgrammingLangu
ages.txt")
   while not s.EndOfStream do yield s.ReadLine() }
```

And just like any other sequence, you can print the data by using the `printfn` method:

```
> data |> printfn "%A";;
seq
  ["C      Dennis MacAlistair Ritchie 1972"; "C++   Bjarne Stroustrup
1985";
   "C#     Anders Hejlsberg    2000"; "F#    Don Syme      2005"; ...]
val it : unit = ()
>
```

OK, now that we have this basic functionality out of our system, let's build something useful using sequences such as an XSV enumerator that iterates through a file in different ways. Since the file is tab-separated (it could be comma-separated or semi-colon separated), we will create a method called XSVEnumerator.

To build an enumerator, we write the following method XSVEnumerator, which takes filename as input, opens the file, and reads the stream until it encounters the end of file, line by line. It splits the lines by the delimiter (in this case it is the tab character), and then yields it as a member of the sequence.

```
let XSVEnumerator(fileName) =

   seq { use s = System.IO.File.OpenText(fileName)
     while not s.EndOfStream do
     let line = s.ReadLine()
     let tokens = line.Split [|'\t'|]
     yield tokens}
```

The preceding code is fairly simple, and intuitive. It is quite similar to how a procedural implementation may also look like. Now that we have our sequence of tokens, let's proceed with trying out different ways of enumerating it:

```
let filename = @"ProgrammingLanguages.txt"

let xsv = XSVEnumerator(filename)
```

When preceded by the @ symbol, the literal value becomes a verbatim string, that is, any escape sequences are ignored.

The first approach is to iterate through the file and to retrieve the array of strings as follows:

```
xsv |> Seq.iter (string >> printfn "line %s");;


>
line System.String[]
<snip>
line System.String[]
val it : unit = ()
```

The second type of enumeration we can perform using `seq.iter` is to determine how many tokens there are in each line. This can be done by checking the length of each line's array. Since we know there are three fields in the file, the result will always be three entries in a line.

```
xsv |> Seq.iter (Array.length >> printfn "line has %d entries");;


>
line has 3 entries
<snip>
line has 3 entries
val it : unit = ()
```

Another enumeration will be to determine the length of each entry. In order to do this, we will perform the length method on each and every element of the array as follows:

```
xsv |> Seq.iter (Array.map (fun s -> s.Length) >> printfn "lengths of
entries: %A");;


>
lengths of entries: [|1; 26; 4|]
lengths of entries: [|3; 17; 4|]
<snip>
lengths of entries: [|5; 14; 4|]
val it : unit = ()
>
```

Last but not least, to see the entire file, we can apply the `ToString()` method on every entry as seen next:

```
xsv |> Seq.iter (Array.map (fun s -> s.ToString()) >> printfn
"Entries: %A")
Entries: [|"C"; "Dennis MacAlistair Ritchie"; "1972"|]
```

```
<snip>
Entries: [|"Scala"; "Martin Odersky"; "2003"|]
val it : unit = ()
```

The preceding example tries to show one way of reading and processing text files using F#. The recommended way of dealing with a data source in F# is using a type provider. Introduced in F# 3.0, there are four built-in type providers to access data from databases and web services. This includes **LINQ-to-SQL**, **SQL Entity**, **Web Services Description Language** (**WSDL**), and **Open Data Protocol** (**OData**). You can write your own type providers but this is beyond the scope of this book.

Query expressions

To retrieve a selective number of elements through a sequence, or page through the sequence, a **query expression** is used. Query expressions allow us to query a data source and put the results in the desired form. Query expressions provide support for LINQ in F#. A typical use case of pagination is a retail location grid where we see 10-20 stores at a time, based on search criteria. This search of elements can later be expanded based on users' selection of the page number.

As a computation expression, query expressions are similar to sequences. Just like sequences, where to populate a sequence you provide code in a sequence expression, for query expression you specify a predicate, a selection query, or similar code.

To understand query expressions, we will expand upon the datasets used in the preceding file and see some examples. Let's begin by creating a type as follows:

1. **Programming Language**: To hold the collection of programming language and the year in which they were first published.

   ```
   type ProgrammingLanguage = { id : int; name : string; publishYear
   : int}
     override x.ToString() = sprintf "%s (%i)" x.name x.publishYear
   ```

2. **Developer type**: To hold the name of the developer who originally developed the programming language.

   ```
   type Developer = { id : int; Name : string  }
     override x.ToString() = sprintf "%s" x.Name
   ```

3. The gerund (or joining/association table for non-Codd fans) that establishes the relationship between developer and programming language:

   ```
   type Developer_PL = { developerID : int; pl_ID : int }
   ```

4. Using these types, let's populate the lists with the corresponding data:

```
let ProgrammingLanguages =
    [
        { id = 1; name = "C"; publishYear = 1972; }
        { id = 2; name = "C++"; publishYear = 1985; }
        { id = 3; name = "C#"; publishYear = 2000; }
        { id = 4; name = "F#"; publishYear = 2005; }
        { id = 5; name = "Java"; publishYear = 1991; }
        { id = 6; name = "Pascal"; publishYear = 1970; }
        { id = 7; name = "Python"; publishYear = 1997; }
        { id = 8; name = "Basic"; publishYear = 1964; }
        { id = 9; name = "COBOL"; publishYear = 1959; }
        { id = 10; name = "FORTRAN"; publishYear = 1957; }
        { id = 11; name = "LISP"; publishYear = 1956; }
        { id = 12; name = "Perl"; publishYear = 1987; }
        { id = 13; name = "JavaScript"; publishYear = 1995; }
        { id = 14; name = "Scheme"; publishYear = 1975; }
        { id = 15; name = "Clojure"; publishYear = 2007; }
        { id = 16; name = "Haskell"; publishYear = 1990; }
        { id = 17; name = "Ruby"; publishYear = 1995; }
        { id = 18; name = "OCaml"; publishYear = 1996; }
        { id = 19; name = "Scala"; publishYear = 2003; }]

let Developers =
    [
        { id = 1; Name = "Dennis Ritchie"; }
        { id = 2; Name = "Bjarne Stroustrup";}
        { id = 3; Name = "Anders Hejlsberg";}
        { id = 4; Name = "Don Syme";}
        { id = 5; Name = "James A. Gosling";}
        { id = 6; Name = "Nicklaus Wirth";}
        { id = 7; Name = "Guido van Rossum";}
        { id = 8; Name = "Kemeny and Kurtz";}
        { id = 9; Name = "Grace Hopper";}
        { id = 10; Name = "John Backus";}
        { id = 11; Name = "John McCarthy";}
        { id = 12; Name = "Larry Wall";}
        { id = 13; Name = "Brendan Eich";}
        { id = 14; Name = "Steele and Sussman";}
        { id = 15; Name = "Rich Hickey";}
        { id = 16; Name = "Jones, Augustsson, et al";}
        { id = 17; Name = "Yukihiro Matsumoto, et al";}
        { id = 18; Name = "Xavier Leroy et al.";}
```

```
                { id = 19; Name = "Martin Odersky";}]

    let Developers_PLs =
      [
        { developerID = 1; pl_ID  = 1; }
        { developerID = 2; pl_ID  = 2; }
        { developerID = 3; pl_ID  = 3; }
        { developerID = 4; pl_ID  = 4; }
        { developerID = 5; pl_ID  = 5; }
        { developerID = 6; pl_ID  = 6; }
        { developerID = 7; pl_ID  = 7; }
        { developerID = 8; pl_ID  = 8; }
        { developerID = 9; pl_ID  = 9; }
        { developerID = 10; pl_ID  = 10; }
        { developerID = 11; pl_ID  = 11; }
        { developerID = 12; pl_ID  = 12; }
        { developerID = 13; pl_ID  = 13; }
        { developerID = 14; pl_ID  = 14; }
        { developerID = 15; pl_ID  = 15; }
        { developerID = 16; pl_ID  = 16; }
        { developerID = 17; pl_ID  = 17; }
        { developerID = 18; pl_ID  = 18; }
        { developerID = 19; pl_ID  = 19 ;}]
```

Now, based on these lists, we can perform simple query operations such as finding out the books published in the year 2005. If you are familiar with LINQ in C#, this syntax will look very similar to you:

```
query { for pl in ProgrammingLanguages do
  where (pl.publishYear = 2005)
  select (pl.ToString()) }

> val it : seq<string> = seq ["F# (2005)"]
```

As you have noticed, in the query expressions, the select keyword performs the same function as yield does in a sequence expression. Along with the select keyword, F# supports a variety of query operators that look very similar to SQL SELECT statements. However, our main interest here is to figure out how to do paging using the query. For this purpose, we use the skip and take operators of the query expression:

```
let getPLPageBySize pageSize pageNumber =
  query { for pl in ProgrammingLanguages do
    skip (pageSize * (pageNumber - 1))
    take pageSize
    select (pl.ToString())}
```

Therefore, if we want to request page #2 of the list and have four elements per page (our page numbers start from 1), the page elements will be requested through the following expression:

```
getPLPageBySize 4 2
val it : seq<string> =
  seq ["Java (1991)"; "Pascal (1970)"; "Python (1997)"; "Basic (1964)"]
```

Let us now stop and take a minute to look at this query expression statement. This is an example to help us appreciate how terse, elegant, and highly readable F# syntax is. Using the same operators, the page can be further sorted by the publishing year in the following query expression:

```
let getPLPageByYear year =
  query { for pl in ProgrammingLanguages do
    sortBy pl.publishYear
    skipWhile (pl.publishYear < year)
    takeWhile (pl.publishYear = year)
    select (pl.ToString()) }
getPLPageByYear 2007
val it : seq<string> = seq ["Clojure (2007)"]
```

It goes without saying that, since we are just operating on the same year, sorting doesn't make much difference. The preceding expression above is functionally equivalent to the next one:

```
    let getPLPageByYear year =
      query { for pl in ProgrammingLanguages do
        where (pl.publishYear = year)
        select (pl.ToString()) }
```

The intent here is to show the power of query expressions and how various SQL-like operations and filters such as `skipWhile`, `takeWhile`, and `Sortby` can be applied.

Query expressions are quite adaptable, and provide various options including an aggregate such as count:

```
query { for f in ProgrammingLanguages do count }
```

```
> val it : int = 19
```

And generic SQL-like selections based on specific parameters such as:

```
query { for pl in ProgrammingLanguages do
    select pl.publishYear  }
```

```
> val it : seq<int> = seq [1972; 1985; 2000; 2005; ..]
```

You have the ability to access `nth` elements:

```
query { for dev in Developers do nth 2 }
```

```
> val it : Developer = {id = 3;
  Name = "Anders Hejlsberg";}
```

You can also aggregate operations such as group by using the appropriate aggregate elements in the select clause as follows:

```
query { for pl in ProgrammingLanguages do
  groupBy pl.publishYear into pl
  sortBy pl.Key
  select (pl.Key, pl) }
```

```
> val it : seq<int * System.Linq.IGrouping<int,ProgrammingLanguage>> =
  seq
    [(1956, seq [{id = 11;
    name = "LISP";
    publishYear = 1956;}]); (1957, seq [{id = 10;
     name = "FORTRAN";
    publishYear = 1957;}]);
     (1959, seq [{id = 9;
    name = "COBOL";
    publishYear = 1959;}]); (1964, seq [{id = 8;
     name = "Basic";
     publishYear = 1964;}]);
  ...]
```

Creating sequences from collections

Any collection that implements `IEnumerable` is fairly easy to convert to a sequence. This is because, by definition, `IEnumerable` is a sequence in F#. Since strings and arrays implement `IEnumerable`, they can be processed without any explicit conversion into functions by using the casting operators on a sequence as seen next:

```
let seqFromArray = [| 1 .. 10 |] :> seq<int>
let seqFromArray = [| 1 .. 10 |] |> Seq.ofArray
```

> The challenge here might be in a case when such functions return a sequence; you may need to convert the returned elements back into an array using `Array.ofSeq` or `Seq.toArray`.

You also see the type casting operators in the preceding statements. The operator `:>` converts a type to another type that is higher in the hierarchy. Its counterpart, the `:?>` operator, converts a type to a different type that is lower in the hierarchy.

Usage considerations for sequences

As seen earlier, sequences help solve problems in a functional manner by helping you avoid imperative constructs such as iterations and accumulators. However, sequences shouldn't be treated like silver bullets and must be used with good judgement, balancing performance and scalability. Recurring evaluation is a performance concern in sequences; even though on-demand evaluation is one of the powerful aspects of sequences, it may become a performance nightmare if you evaluate all the elements more than once. Depending on the sequence expression, you may end up paying a performance price for evaluating each element many times. In case you need to pre-calculate all the elements ahead of time, you can opt to use a different data structure or apply `Seq.cache` to the sequence.

Along with performance, a developer must also address the non-functional requirements of debugging, readability, and maintainability. Since sequences are evaluated in a lazy manner, it is hard to decipher whether certain operations were actually invoked. When stepping through code, this can result in an awful debugging experience. This can be overcome by mapping the sequence into another data structure such as an array using `Array.ofSeq`.

> A hidden secret of F# sequences is that they are monads. Monads or computation builders are functional constructs that include a specific set of laws that govern their operation. In plain English, you can think of monads as a boundary around a type or as a type enhancer. Sequences are a context around computations (and values) and this context can be propagated. For instance, in the following sequence of values:
>
> ```
> let values = seq { for x in 0..9 -> x = x * x},
> ```
>
> The context under which the sequence is generated is encapsulated in the expression along with a yield statement that serves as return.

Summary

This chapter was a deep dive into the ubiquitous `IEnumerable`, the F# data structure of sequences. Now, you should have a thorough understanding of sequences, the underlying operations, and query expressions. A sequence is a list of *potential* values computed on demand. Sequences can be created using a range expression, a sequence expression, the `seq` keyword, library methods such as `init` and `initInfinite` from the `Seq` module, or simply by treating some `IEnumerable` as an F# sequence. The `Seq` module has a large number of sequence-related operations available. You can easily implement custom enumeration (paging) in sequences by applying predicate-based filters. Last, but not the least, you should optimize the evaluations in the sequence and use `Seq.cache` to avoid repeated evaluation whenever possible.

In the next chapter, we will gain knowledge about a custom ADT, which is outside the F# core library—a stack. You will also be prepared for more advanced implementations, necessary test cases (the F# approach to unit testing), and finally simple algorithms using stacks. We will implement balanced symbols (that is, bracket matching) to demonstrate the stack concepts in action.

Let's Stack Up

5

"Whereas some declarative programmers only pay lip service to equational reasoning, users of functional languages exploit them every time they run a compiler, whether they notice it or not."

– Philip Wadler, How to Declare an Imperative

In the last chapter, we delved into the ubiquitous `IEnumerable <T>` and sequence type (`Seq <T>`) which is the alias for it. In this chapter, we shift our focus to another essential data structure, the `stack`. Stacks, heaps, hash tables, and linked lists are some of the fundamental data structures used in everyday development. In this chapter, we will gain knowledge about stacks by building one as a custom **Abstract Data Type** (**ADT**), which is outside the F# core library. Having an in-depth understanding of stack will prepare you for further, more advanced implementations. We will explore the operations which our implementation requires, necessary test cases, and finally, simple algorithms using stacks, such as converting decimal numbers to binary representations and in-fix/post-fix notations for balancing symbols (brackets matching) — good interview questions! In this chapter, we will also see the F# approach to unit testing for the first time.

In this chapter, we will cover the following topics:

* Definition and implementation of a stack ADT
* Building stack with concurrency support
* Getting started with unit testing in F# using MSTest and NUnit
* Testing a stack implementation using MSTest and NUnit
* Building algorithms using the stack balancing expression parenthesis

Let's build a stack

Stacks (also known as pushdown stacks) are simple, last-in-first-out data structures. The **LIFO (Last-In-First-Out)** policy of this data structure distinguishes it from the queues which follow the **FIFO (First-In-First-Out)** paradigm. A stack allows you to add and remove items by pushing and popping them off respectively. Some of the typical stack methods are as follows:

```
Pushdown (LIFO) stack


              Stack()                create an empty stack
      void    push(Item item)       add an item
      Item    pop()                 remove the most recently added item
   boolean    isEmpty()             is the stack empty?
       int    size()                number of items in the stack
```

A typical modern day example of stack is a web browser where all the links are stored on a stack. When you press the back button (the metaphorical arch-nemesis of a web developer), it pops the last visited item in the sequence which is retrieved and so on and so forth. In this ordered collection of items, removals and the additions always occur from the same end point, that is, the top of the stack, contrary to the opposite end, the base. Therefore, by definition, the items closest to the base have been in the stack the longest.

As we saw in the last chapter, building an **Abstract Data Type (ADT)** requires us to implement the methods to represent the inherent functionality and storage policy of the type. In the case of stack, we can start by implementing the following basic methods:

- `Stack()`: Creates a new empty stack
- `Push (<item>)`: Adds a new item to the top of the stack
- `Pop()`: Removes the top item from the stack

As you noticed, since the stack gets modified, this is not going to be an immutable structure and F# does not provide a built-in implementation of stack. Also, our first implementation will not guarantee thread safety.

The built-in List data type in F# is an ordered, immutable series of elements of the same type which makes it a perfect candidate to create the underlying structure to build a stack upon. So we can start by declaring the following parameterized type definition to create a stack of generic elements:

```
type Stack<'T>() =
  -let mutable _stack : List<'T> = []
```

This declares a Stack ADT with a mutable instance of List for us which will be used to store the stack elements. The ' operator defines a generic type parameter. Before we start implementing the essential push and pop methods, let's do a quick refresher in pattern matching which we will heavily use in these methods.

We have discussed pattern matching and active patterns earlier. A simple switch case statement with pattern matching looks like the following code snippet. You will see this pattern matching style widely used in F#:

```
let PickProgrammingParadigm (x : int) =
  match x with
  | 1 -> "Imperative"
  | 2 -> "Procedural"
  | 3 -> "Declarative"
  | 4 -> "Functional"
  | 5 -> "Object Oriented"
  | 6 -> "Event Driven"
  | 7 -> "Automata Based"
  | _ -> x.ToString()
```

When you run this statement in FSI with an undefined argument, it matches the last line, that is, catches all and prints the string:

```
> PickProgrammingParadigm -1;;
val it : string = "-1"
```

Similarly for a known case, you would see the value of the typed int:

```
> PickProgrammingParadigm 4;;
>
val it : string = "Functional"
```

Another, similar pattern matching example for different cases is how you can compare an array. For instance, here you can see matching expressions against different types of arrays along with the catch-all expression:

```
let MatchArray arr =
  match arr with
  | [||] -> "An Empty Array"
```

```
    | [|x|] -> sprintf "Single Value: %A" x
    | [|x;y|] -> sprintf "A Pair: %A and %A" x y
    | _ -> sprintf ">2 Array"
```

When you pass an array with three elements to the matching expression, it matches the catch-all and prints accordingly:

```
> MatchArray [| 1; 2; 3|];;
val it : string = ">2 Array"
```

F# is quite efficient about letting you know if your matching expression has any issues, that is, if it won't match all the cases and so on. Like array, you can also match lists. The syntax is similar to arrays but with lists, you operate using heads and tail with the cons operator. The cons :: operator in F# prepends elements to the list and also works as a pattern matching operator (which is how it is being used in the following example) to split the head element and the tail (after removing the head or everything after the head):

```
let MatchList list =
  match list with
  | [] -> "An Empty List"
  | head::tail -> sprintf "List %A has %i more elements" head (tail.
Length)
```

A little bit regarding the :: operator in the context of lists: since F# lists are singly linked and immutable, it is feasible to create the new element in the front through cons ::. Singly linked lists contain nodes with the next field pointing to the next node, in contrast to a doubly linked list which also has a previous-node pointer. The dynamic nature of linked lists comes from the fact that instead of replicating the entire list, you can just create an element and point it to the existing list. You can also use the @ operator to append an element to the back but it would be computationally expensive, and therefore is considered bad practice (or code smell).

The .NET **FCL (Framework Class Library)** provides us with System.Collections. Stack, which can be used in F#; our implementation of the stack is a much stricter structure than the one provided with the framework. It is also important to note that in this implementation, we will be using the following pattern matching syntax along with the cons operator to take the top element off the stack, and assign the remainder back to the stack:

```
match test-expression with
    | pattern1 [ when condition ] -> result-expression1
    | pattern2 [ when condition ] -> result-expression2
    | ...
```

Pattern matching has a learning curve but in order to write idiomatic F#, you would need to get comfortable with it.

Now to begin with the stack implementation, we will only support two basic operations; pushing elements onto the stack, and popping them off again.

A `Push` function will be defined as follows:

```
member this.Push value =
  _stack <- value :: _stack
```

This `Push` member function is defined to append the new value with the existing stack, and then assign it to the stack variable.

In case of pop, we need to define it so it returns the top value from the stack, and also removes it from the stack.

As you can see in the `Pop` method, we take the element (result) out of the stack, assign the entire remainder back to the stack, and return the result element. Here, the `cons` operator splits the internal list into the first item, and the remainder. Then we proceed to mutate the internal list, that is, assign the value, to be just the remainder, before returning that first element:

```
member this.Pop =
  match _stack with
  | result :: remainder ->
    _stack <- remainder
    result
  | [] -> failwith "Stack is Empty"
```

The `failwith` function is used to perform exception handling in F#. If the stack is empty, we fail with the `Stack is Empty` message and the exception (`Microsoft.FSharp.Core.FailureException`). The code looks quite simple but writing this idiomatic style F# intuitively comes with practice and reading functionality style code. Notice that the code does not have verbose `if` statements, or explicit checks. The expressions for concatenation, assignments, and return statements appear subtly, in a terse and formal manner.

Now that we have a basic stack implemented, let's do some pushing and popping. First we will create an instance of the `stack` type with `string`:

```
> let stack = Stack<string>();;
val stack : Stack<string>
```

Let's push an epigram here, word by word—`Syntactic sugar causes cancer of semicolon`:

```
> stack.Push("Syntactic");;
val it : unit = ()
> stack.Push("sugar");;
```

```
val it : unit = ()
> stack.Push("causes");;
val it : unit = ()
> stack.Push("cancer");;
val it : unit = ()
> stack.Push("of");;
val it : unit = ()
> stack.Push("semicolon");;
val it : unit = ()
```

Now when we start popping this out, you would see that the last element gets popped out first, and so on and so forth:

```
> stack.Pop();;
val it : string = "semicolon"
> stack.Pop();;
val it : string = "of"
> stack.Pop();;
val it : string = "cancer"
> stack.Pop();;
val it : string = "causes"
> stack.Pop();;
val it : string = "sugar"
> stack.Pop();;
val it : string = "Syntactic"
```

This happens until the stack is empty. If I try to pop it one more time, I get the following error:

```
> stack.Pop();;
System.Exception: Stack is Empty
  at FSI_0062.Stack`1.Pop[a](a value) in HelloWorld\Stacks.fs:line 14
  at <StartupCode$FSI_0077>.$FSI_0077.main@()
```

Now the question is, how to avoid this from happening, or how to make the Pop operation handle the empty stack condition gracefully? The answer is building a TryPop method. This method will be very similar to Pop method except for the use of Some and None:

```
member this.TryPop =
  match _stack with
  | result :: remainder ->
    _stack <- remainder
    result |> Some
  | [] -> None
```

As you recall, the `option` type in F# allows us to handle the exception if the value for a variable doesn't exist. For instance, we can say:

```
let exists (x : int option) =
  match x with
  | Some(x) -> true
  | None -> false
```

In which case, the value is returned if it exists, otherwise it will return none. We could have written the `result |> Some` as `Some` (result) but it is neither idiomatic, nor nearly as cool-looking. Let's experiment with this new `TryPop`:

```
> let stack = new Stack<string>();;
> stack.Push ("hello");;
> stack.Push ("world");;

> stack.Pop;;
val it : string = "world"
> stack.Pop;;
val it : string = "hello"
> stack.Pop;;
> System.Exception: Stack is Empty
> stack.TryPop;;
val it : string option = None
```

This method allows us to maintain the integrity of the stack and keep the failures graceful. As you noticed, this entire implementation is not thread-safe; that is, if there are multiple threads using this instance, it can potentially have incorrect or out-of-sync data. There are concurrent thread-safe collections in the .NET Framework base class library which can be used to replace our existing use of list. Also, to simplify, we can use F# lock statements around anything which involves reading or writing the internal list structure. This will protect the integrity of the data in case another thread comes in and mutates the structure while it's being used.

Stack with concurrency support

Building upon the earlier implementation of stack, here is a simple implementation of a concurrent stack where we use the `lock` keyword to stop any other thread from using the variable while it is in use. By obtaining the mutual-exclusion lock, the `lock` keyword marks a statement block as a critical section. The lock is released after the statement is executed. The following example includes a lock statement to support concurrency. The `lock` keyword signature follows.

```
lock : 'Lock -> (unit -> 'T) -> 'T (requires reference type)
```

To make this stack thread safe, we use `lock` to allow the execution of the function in a critical section. The unit is the action which needs to be performed:

```
type ConcurrentStack<'T>() =
  let mutable _stack : List<'T> = []

  member this.Push value =
    lock _stack (fun () ->
      _stack <- value :: _stack)

  member this.Pop() =
    lock _stack (fun () ->
      match _stack with
      | result :: remainder ->
      _stack <- remainder
      result
      | [] -> failwith "Empty stack"
  )
```

By locking the stack which is the underlying collection, no other thread will be allowed to modify the contents of the list until the critical section operation is completed by the current thread.

It is crucial to consider thread safety in programming multi-threaded applications, especially when you are building data structures, because these errors are very hard to debug and very easy to ignore as they don't happen during development. Fault isolation and atomicity are key tenets to scalability when your applications are under stress in a real-world environment.

Testing the stack

This is your first introduction to unit testing in F# and requires some familiarity with unit testing frameworks (NUnit, MSTest), as well as NuGet, the .NET Package Manager. You have been working with **FSI (FSharp Interactive)** within the Visual Studio lately. In this section, we are going to exploit more features of Visual Studio than of REPL.

In order to test the stack methods, `Push` and `Pop`, you need to create a test project. Let's first exploit the cross-language functionality provided by **MSIL (Microsoft Intermediate Language** or **IL)** and write our first unit tests in C#. Being a member of the .NET family of languages, F#, like C#, and VB.NET, eventually gets translated to IL before it is executed. That is why it is easy to write libraries and classes in any of these languages and use them in others in a seamless manner, most of the time. To demonstrate this, we will use C# and MSTest to write a test case for the stack that we have created in F#.

To write a test case, you would need to add a test project to your existing solution. You can do this by right-clicking on your solution in the **Solution Explorer** (typically on the right side), and then selecting **Add | New Project | Unit Test Project** from Visual Studio IDE.

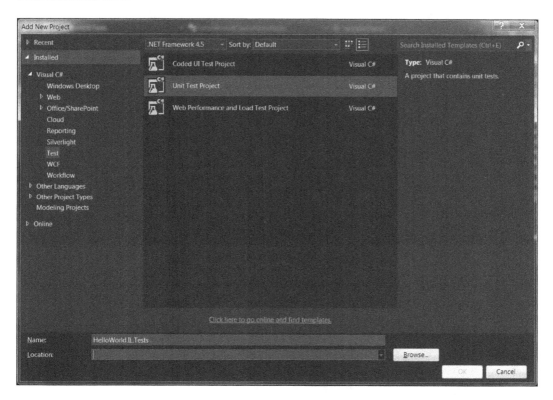

Once you complete this step, the unit test project will appear as a part of your solution. Now you need to create a `test` method to verify the functionality of the stack. However, before you do this, you would need to add a reference to the original `Stacks` project so that your test project actually has a reference to what it is trying to test.

In order to do that, you can right-click on the test project, select **Add** from the sub menu, and then select **Reference** as shown in the next screenshot:

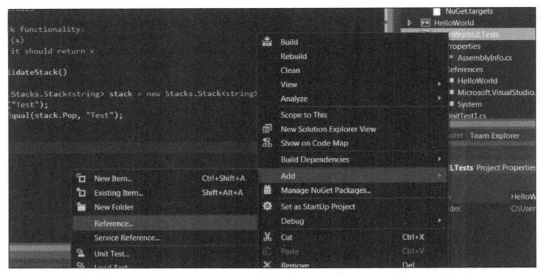

Adding a reference to the original stack project

This will pop up the following dialogue box from where you can add the references from the projects which are part of the solution:

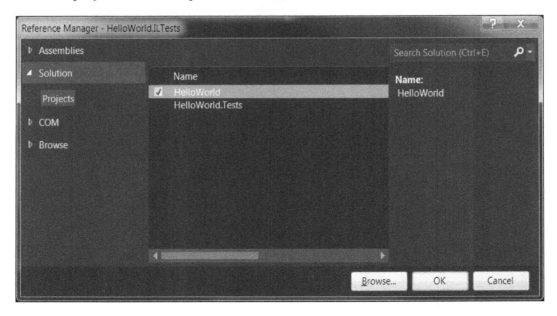

Click **OK** and the `Stacks` project reference is now part of your unit testing project. You can read more about adding and removing projects, and the DLL references on MSDN at `http://msdn.microsoft.com/en-us/library/wkze6zky.aspx`.

Now that our project is all set for testing out the stack, let's write our first unit test to validate the stack's functionality:

```
using System;
using Microsoft.VisualStudio.TestTools.UnitTesting;

namespace HelloWorld.ILTests
{
  [TestClass]
  public class FSUnitTests
  {
    //validate stack functionality:
    //push element (x)
    //pop element: it should return x
    [TestMethod]
    public void validateStack()
    {
      HelloWorld.Stacks.Stack<string> stack = new Stacks.
Stack<string>();
      stack.Push("Test");
      Assert.AreEqual(stack.Pop, "Test");
    }
  }
}
```

The preceding test is fairly intuitive even if you are not too familiar with the C# syntax. In the first line, we create an instance of the stack:

```
HelloWorld.Stacks.Stack<string> stack = new Stacks.Stack<string>();
```

You can also write this line as follows:

```
var stack = new Stacks.Stack<string>();
```

But for the sake of better readability, I chose explicit declaration. Now that we have an instance defined, you can invoke the `Push` method:

```
stack.Push("Test");
```

Based on the implementation, we know that string `Test` now lives on the stack. Therefore, a valid test is to ensure that it actually exists by popping the stack:

```
Assert.AreEqual(stack.Pop, "Test");
```

By asserting that the value returned is same as the `Test`, we can test the stack's functionality. In the following screenshot, you can see the method in action where the left-hand side pane (**Test Explorer**) shows you that the unit test executed successfully:

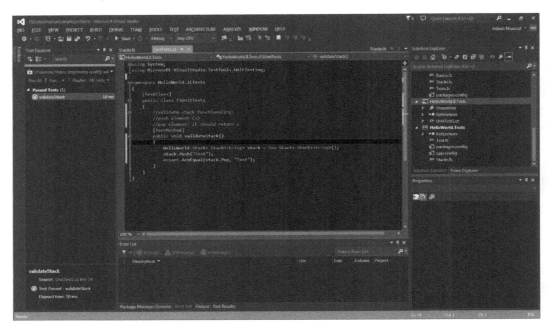

You can read more about the Assert class and its methods on MSDN at `http://msdn.microsoft.com/en-us/library/Microsoft.VisualStudio.TestTools.UnitTesting.Assert.aspx`. Now that we have demonstrated how to test an F# method using MSTest and C#, we can go a little puritan and do the same using F#.

At this point, you will need to create a separate F# project for unit testing which we will name `HelloWorld.Tests`. It can just be a library project since, unfortunately, there is no built-in unit testing template available for F# at the time of writing this book. You can download one from Code Project for Visual Studio 2012 at `https://visualstudiogallery.msdn.microsoft.com/432eb82c-345e-4502-be56-015fe051a210`. However, since we are using VS.NET 2013 for these examples, we will refrain from using this template.

The good news is that you can still test using **MSTest** as long as you are using the right testing attributes. You can also use a more accessible tool, **NUnit**. Let's see how all this works.

If you are not familiar with NuGet, it is the package manager for .NET. It allows developers to create and consume packages, and provides a central packaging repository. You can start the package manager in Visual Studio IDE from the **Tools** Menu:

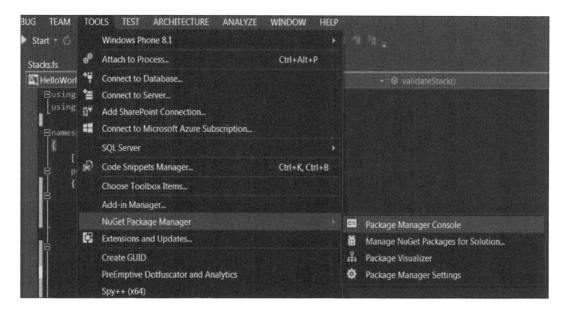

Once you have the package manager console started, you can use it to install the packages. For example, in this case we will be installing the NUnit by invoking the following **Package Manager Console** install command:

```
Each package is licensed to you by its owner. Microsoft is not
responsible for, nor does it grant any licenses to, third-party packages.
Some packages may include dependencies which are governed by additional
licenses. Follow the package source (feed) URL to determine any
dependencies.

Package Manager Console Host Version 2.8.50926.663

Type 'get-help NuGet' to see all available NuGet commands.

PM> install-package Nunit
Installing 'NUnit 2.6.4'.
Successfully installed 'NUnit 2.6.4'.
Adding 'NUnit 2.6.4' to HelloWorld.
Successfully added 'NUnit 2.6.4' to HelloWorld.
```

Other frequently used commands in NuGet include `Find-Package` (for NuGet 3.0 Beta client or higher), `Get-Package`, `Get-Project`, `Install-Package`, `Open-PackagePage`, `Sync-Package` (for NuGet 3.0 Beta client or higher), `Uninstall-Package`, and `Update-Package`.

Now that NUnit is a part of your project, you can start by writing a dummy unit test in F# as follows:

```
module HelloWorld.Tests

open NUnit.Framework

[<Test>]
let DoesItSayHello () = Assert.AreEqual("Hello World!", "Hello
World!")
```

This test will appear in the IDE as seen in the following screenshot:

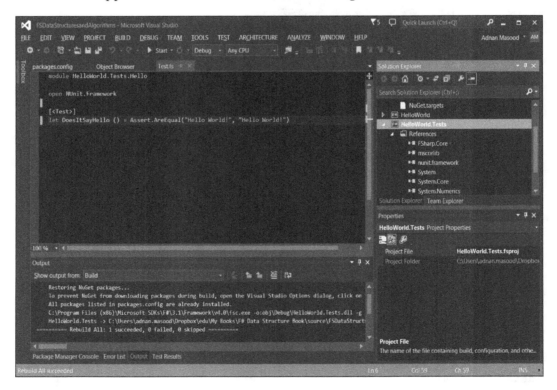

You can test whether this unit test is running effectively by opening up the NUnit console which can be downloaded from `http://www.nunit.org/index.php?p=download`.

Add the assembly to the NUnit console IDE as shown in the following screenshot. The assembly will be located in the `Debug` folder of your test project, that is, `HelloWorld.Tests\bin\Debug`.

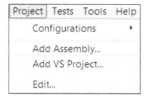

Now you can run the test and see the green bar as seen in the following screenshot:

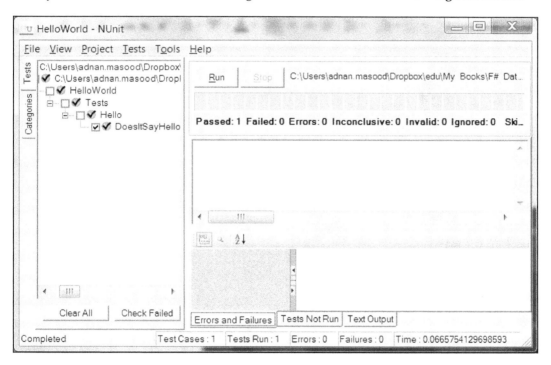

You can use this approach to test your F# stack as well. In order to test, first you need a reference to your original project added to your F# testing library. The process is similar to how we did it for the C# library. Now you can write your unit test as follows:

```
module HelloWorld.Tests.StackTests
open Microsoft.VisualStudio.TestTools.UnitTesting
open HelloWorld.Stacks
```

```
[<TestClass>]
type testrun() =

  [<TestMethod>]
  member x.validateStackFS() =
    let stack = new Stack<string>();
    stack.Push "Hello World"
    Assert.AreEqual ("Hello World", stack.Pop)
```

This test is very similar to the C# test that you saw earlier. The Visual Studio test explorer sees this new test `validateStackFS` and you can run it in the IDE, as well as in the NUnit explorer:

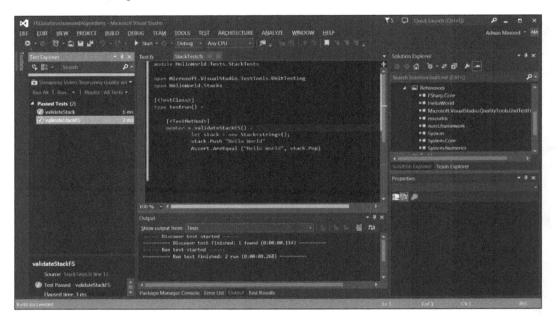

Algorithm – parenthesis matching using stacks

In computer science, stack data structure serves a variety of uses, from operating system function pointer management to compiler construction. We will try to be less ambitious and use the stack to solve the parenthesis matching problem. Instead of using the stack data structure explicitly, we will implicitly use stack operations to show you how to use the stack constructs within the algorithm.

A typical arithmetic expression is usually written as follows:

$$(8+3)*(6+9)/(1-1)$$

Here, the parentheses are being used to provide the order in which the operators will be applied in the statement. Also, in various programming languages, we use different types of brackets to represent scope and an incomplete set of brackets will raise a compiler warning.

For the languages which use them, balancing the sets of opening and closing parenthesis is crucial to manage the scope of variables and methods, as well as explaining the execution context for statements and functions. A matching and balanced instance of parenthesis looks like follows:

$$(()()())$$

$$(()((())()))$$

And unbalanced instance will appear like this:

$$((((((()))$$

$$(()(()$$

With our newly acquired knowledge about stack, we will use the stack data structure to write a program which will identify the correctly balanced parenthesis. The problem we are trying to address requires us to create an algorithm which reads the string of parenthesis (the statement), or in general, different identifiers, and makes sure that the symbols used are balanced, that is, the beginnings and endings must match in proper order.) (is not proper.

If you think about the problem with stack as a storage mechanism, it is just storing a bunch of characters. However, it will become evident that stack is quite an appropriate data structure to store the opening parentheses (push), and remove (pop) whenever there is a closing parenthesis. If, by the end of the expression being processed, we have no elements left in the stack, the statement is balanced.

A simpler, not-so-idiomatic implementation begins with checking for the length of the string:

```
|  []  ->
   if stack.Length > 0 then
     false
   else
      true
```

If the length of the string is greater than 0, and the stack is empty, the string is not really balanced. On the contrary, if the expression and the stack are both empty, this means that the expression was balanced. The balancing method is designed to be recursive, that is, it operates on the input string of parentheses multiple times.

Also in this case of pattern matching, : : can be used as a special pattern matching construct as compared to the usual cons operator used to append lists. This describes head::tail that is, the list has a head (first element), and a tail (remainder).

```
|  x::xs  ->
```

For this core matching case, if the first element is a beginning parenthesis, it is evident to call balance with the tail, and the header element of the stack:

```
if x = '(' then
  balance xs x::stack
```

If the matching element is), that is, the closing parenthesis, you should check if the stack has any elements left:

```
elif x = ')' then
   if stack.Length = 0 then
     false
   else
      stack = stack.tail
```

If the stack has no elements remaining and your string has at least one element left, for example the closing parenthesis, this statement you are processing is not balanced. Therefore you return false as response. Otherwise, you would assign the remainder of the stack to the stack (effectively popping), for further recursion.

Summing up this approach, the idiomatic F# implementation to check if a string of parenthesis is balanced follows:

```
let BalanceExpression expr =
  let rec balancer xs stack =
    match (xs, stack) with
    | [], [] -> true
    | [], _ -> false
    | '(' :: ys,  stack -> balancer ys ('(' :: stack)
    | ')' :: ys, '(' :: stack -> balancer ys stack
    | ')' :: _, _ -> false
    | _ :: ys, stack -> balancer ys stack
  balancer (Seq.toList expr) []
```

Let's step through the implementation. As mentioned earlier, balancer is the recursive function to iterate through the stack. What happens here is that we are using a stack to push when it encounters (, use the : : operator to do the split, and pop when it comes across) in the string. The first condition (should be the final condition in a more idiomatic manner but I moved it upwards for the sake of simplicity) is evidently what you saw in the preceding code. If the string list is empty, the stack may still have an item. We check for the item and return true (balanced) if the list and the stack are both empty.

```
| [], [] -> true
| [], _ -> false
```

If the list is empty but there is still something left on the stack, there is still a balancing problem as seen in the second statement of the preceding code.

Let's test the program by passing in a balanced expression:

```
> BalanceExpression "(())";;
val it : bool = true
```

Similarly, for the unbalanced expression, the values will be `false`:

```
> BalanceExpression "(((( )))";;
val it : bool = false
```

For effective testing, you should write unit tests against these methods. Unit tests are the most effective, repeatable way of ensuring code coverage.

Summary

In this chapter, we covered a lot of ground. We started with building a basic ADT of stack using F# and after implementing the fundamental operations, proceeded to make a concurrent version of stack. Then, step by step, we learned how to do unit testing in C# for an F# program, and how to implement the same test method in F#. Later we used our knowledge of stack operations to implement the parenthesis balancing algorithm.

Continuing with the theme of implementing ADTs, in the next chapter, we will learn about graph related algorithms, and implementation of our own trees. Starting from a simple binary tree, we will discuss how implementation differs for an imperative (mutable) versus persistent structure. Then we will cover balancing and the assessment of amortization cost whilst analyzing an AVL tree implementation and the operations on it. From there we will tackle tree searching and various traversal techniques. This will provide us with an insight into n-trees, balanced trees, searching, traversal methods, and understanding why most of the F# built-in data structures are actually based on trees.

6
See the Forest for the Trees

I will, in fact, claim that the difference between a bad programmer and a good one is whether he considers his code or his data structures more important. Bad programmers worry about the code. Good programmers worry about data structures and their relationships.

– Linus Torvalds

In the previous chapter, we started with building a basic ADT of stack using F# and after implementing the fundamental operations, proceeded to make a concurrent version of stack. Then, step-by-step, we learned how to do unit testing in C# for an F# program, and how to implement the same test method in F#. Later, we used our knowledge of stack operations to implement the parenthesis balancing algorithm.

Continuing with the theme of implementing ADTs, in this chapter we will learn about graph-related algorithms, and implementation of our own trees. Starting with a simple binary tree, we will discuss how implementation differs for an imperative (mutable) versus persistent structure. Then we will cover balancing and the assessment of amortization cost whilst analyzing an AVL tree implementation and the operations on it. From there, we will tackle tree searching and various traversal techniques. This will provide us an insight into n-Trees, balanced trees, searching, traversal methods and an understanding of why most of the F# built-in data structures are actually based on trees.

In this chapter we will cover the following topics:

- Custom implementation of a binary tree
- Navigating a binary tree
- Benefits of tree data structure including fast searching and traversal techniques
- Implementing and analyzing an abstract syntax tree

Tree as a data structure

Trees are everywhere! As a data structure, trees are highly prolific in computer science literature. Due to their ubiquity and powerful intuitive design, in computer science algorithms you would see trees being used in diverse domains. Whether it be file systems, sentence parsing, compiler construction algorithms, or human ancestry solutions, trees can represent hierarchical structures quite effectively.

In computer science, graphs are one of the fundamental data structures used for representing information from web links to metabolic pathways in cells. A graph consists of nodes (also known as vertices) and edges (which is a quite confusing name since they are links and not literally edges). Graphs can also contain cycles. We will discuss graphs in greater detail in *Chapter 8, Quick Boost with Graph.*

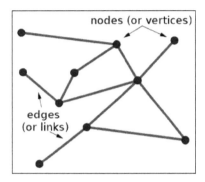

A tree, on the other hand, is a special case of a graph in which any two nodes can be connected by exactly one pathway. This restriction distinguishes trees from the graphs — that no single node can have multiple parents. Directed graphs also allow storing elements (node values) with a parent-child hierarchy. Mentioning this distinction, Skienna writes the following in his seminal work on algorithm design:

> *"An important and honorable technique in algorithm design is to narrow the set of allowable instances until there is a correct and efficient algorithm. For example, we can restrict a graph problem from general graphs down to trees, or a geometric problem from two dimensions down to one."*

> *– Skienna*

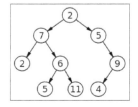

In the preceding figure, you can see that the tree has the following key features:

- The tree has a special node **2**, called the root of the tree, with no parent node
- A parent node is a node which has at least one child
- Nodes with no children of their own, in this case **2, 5, 11**, and **4** are considered leaves or external nodes
- Each node *n* of the tree is different from root node **2** and has a unique parent node

Now our question is, how do we represent a tree in the F# code? Luckily F# excels in the various different ways in which we can represent trees. A simple form would be representing a tree as a recursive data structure, that is, a tree containing a list of trees.

```
type tree = Node of tree list
```

This simplistic F# representation of a tree is called an **n-ary** tree or **n-way** trees. These are trees in which each node may contain up to *n* children. The other two popular types include B-tree or balanced variant of an n-way tree, and B+ tree in which all leaves are connected to provide faster traversal. Like real life, any two nodes which are children of the same parent node are known as siblings. Also, the subtree of a tree is the tree consisting of all the descendants of the child node, therefore a tree within a tree. A tree is considered an ordered tree if there is a way to identify the order of the children of each vertex. Ordered trees are used to represent a linear order relationship between the nodes.

Several data structures in F# and other programming languages are implemented with underlying trees. This is because in contrast with linear data structures such as arrays and linked lists, trees are hierarchical and help in the storage of information such as ranking, tiers, order, classification, and categories. Another reason for using trees is their search effectiveness with $O(log\ n)$ upper bound in case of AVL and red black trees.

Now that you know some of the basic terminology of the trees, let's explore some of the special and popular cases with examples.

The binary search tree

One of the most popular forms of trees in computer science is the binary tree. As the name indicates, a binary tree is a tree in which every node has either zero, one or, at the most, two child nodes. A binary tree is also sometimes referred to as a binary search tree; however, they are different as we show you next.

For example, you can see a binary tree in the diagram that follows, a tree where every node has at most two children:

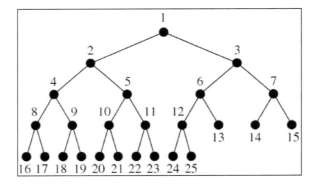

In a binary search tree, the left child node contains only the nodes with values which are less than the parent node. Similarly, the right child node can only contain nodes with values greater than or equal to the parent node as shown in the following figure:

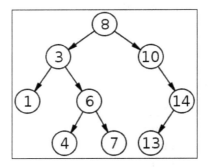

In F#, there are various ways of representing a binary tree. For example, a discriminated union-based binary tree of strings can be written as follows:

```
type tree =
  |Leaf of string
  |Node of tree * tree
```

And a generic version can be as follows:

```
type tree<'a> =
  |Leaf of 'a
  |Node of tree<'a> * tree<'a>
```

A (height) balanced binary tree is a tree where among any two leaves, the difference of the depth is at most one. It can be represented by the following list-based recursive function:

```
let rec bal_tree = function
    | 0 -> Node []
    | n ->
      Node [bal_tree(n-1); bal_tree (n-1)];;
```

Depth of a node is defined as the number of edges from the node to the tree's root node. In contrast, the height of a node is defined as the number of edges on the longest path from the node to a leaf. A root node has a depth of 0 while a leaf node has a height of 0.

The `bal_tree` function in the preceding code, applies to the node containing two balanced binary trees of depth $n-1$. You can create a balanced tree of two nodes each as follows:

```
> let btree = bal_tree 2;;
```

```
val btree : tree = Node [Node [Node []; Node []]; Node [Node []; Node
[]]]
```

```
F# Interactive
type tree = | Node of tree list

>

val bal_tree : _arg1:int -> tree

>
> let btree = bal_tree 2;;

val btree : tree = Node [Node [Node []; Node []]; Node [Node []; Node []]]
```

Traversing a tree and identifying nodes is fairly easy in this structure. An example would be counting the leaf nodes, that is, the nodes which have no more children. It can be accomplished by using the following `fold` operation:

```
let rec CountLeafNodes = function
    | Node [] -> 1
    | Node list ->
      Seq.fold (fun s t -> s + CountLeafNodes t) 0 list
```

When we run this against the tree created in the preceding code snippet, following is the result:

```
>
> CountLeafNodes btree;;
val it : int = 4
```

Now let's review some of the tree traversal techniques and how we can implement these in F#.

Navigating the tree

Consider the tree in the following figure. Our objective is to traverse the tree, that is, iterate through the nodes. There are several different approaches to do so but some of the most common ones are in-order, post-order, and pre-order traversal:

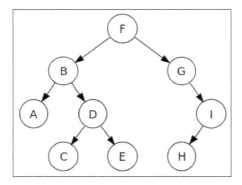

In the in-order traversal, we start from the root node and traverse to left subtree, and then we visit the root node and then traverse to right subtree as seen in the following. The nodes are traversed in this order: **A, B, C, D, ..., H, I**:

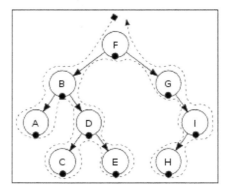

An in-order traversal algorithm can be implemented in F# as the following recursive function. In this function, we utilize the power of sequences, and the `match` expressions to implement the in-order traversal algorithm:

```
type Tree<'a> =
    | Tree of 'a * Tree<'a> * Tree<'a>
    | Leaf of 'a

let rec inorder tree =
  seq {
    match tree with
      | Tree(x, left, right) ->
      yield! inorder left
      yield x
      yield! inorder right
    | Leaf x -> yield x
  }
```

As you have aptly noted by now, the preceding code looks very much like the algorithm it implements with the effective use of `yield!`, the F# keyword to return a subsequence, merged into the final sequence. It operates on the left and the right nodes recursively until the leaf nodes are reached, and output during this process. Take a look at the following example:

```
let mytree = Tree("D", Tree("B", Leaf("A"), Leaf("C")), Leaf("E"))

let myseq = inorder mytree

printfn "%A" myseq
```

The output of the tree definition and the in-order traversal follows:

```
type Tree<'a> =
  | Tree of 'a * Tree<'a> * Tree<'a>
  | Leaf of 'a
val inorder : tree:Tree<'a> -> seq<'a>
val mytree : Tree<string> = Tree ("D",Tree ("B",Leaf "A",Leaf "C"),Leaf "E")
val myseq : seq<string>
val it : unit = ()

>
```

In pre-order traversal, we start with the root node, traverse to left subtree and then traverse to right subtree (node **F**, **B**, **A**, **D**) as seen in the following figure:

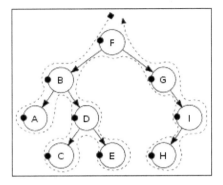

Similar to the in-order traversal, the pre-order traversal can be performed as follows in F#. If you look closely, the significant difference lies in the order of expression, that is, root node, then left and right:

```
let rec preorder tree =
  seq {
    match tree with
      | Tree(x, left, right) ->
        yield x
        yield! preorder left
        yield! preorder right
      | Empty -> ()
  }
```

Last but not the least, we have the post-order traversal in which we start with the left subtree, traverse it to the right subtree and then traverse to the root node as seen in the following figure:

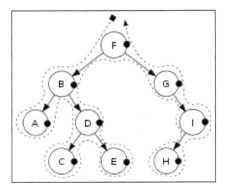

Now, let's look at the following:

```
let rec postorder tree =
  seq {
    match tree with
      | Tree(x, left, right) ->
        yield! postorder left
        yield! postorder right
        yield x
    | Empty -> ()
  }
```

Besides the traversal types discussed here, there are breadth- and depth-first searches used when searching the tree. The depth-first search is the same as in-order traversal with a criteria to terminate when the item is found. The breadth-first search is however, slightly different and can be best implemented by using a Stack to help with the search.

Eliminating the need of backtracking, depth-first search visits all vertices in the graph that are *k* edges (links), far from the source node before visiting any node that is *k+1* links away. As the name of the search algorithm suggests, this process explores the depth and repeats it until there are no more nodes reachable from the starting node. In the breadth-first search, we begin by enqueuing the root node and repeat the following process:

- De-queue a node in the stack
- If the node-element = Search-Element
  - Terminate the search and return
  - Else, enqueue all the undiscovered child nodes
- If Queue = Empty, terminate the search since the element cannot be found
  - Else repeat from the first step

Try to implement this algorithm in F#; we have provided a solution in the accompanying code.

Abstract syntax trees

Abstract syntax trees (AST) are the tree representations of the symbolic expressions in programming languages. F# can provide an elegant representation of symbolic expressions as trees. In order to evaluate an expression tree, we need to traverse it in post-order. A simple expression tree for the statement $1+2*3$ can be represented as follows:

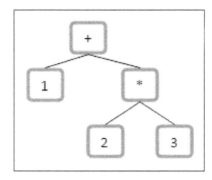

Like the mathematical expression tree (a specialized abstraction syntax tree) in the preceding example, an expression in a programming language is typically composed of variables and operators.

```
type expression =
    | Integer of int
    | Var of string
    | Addition of expression * expression
    | Multiply of expression * expression ;;
```

Therefore, the expression tree for the statement $1+2*3$ can be represented as follows:

```
type expression =
    | Integer of int
    | Var of string
    | Addition of expression * expression
    | Multiply of expression * expression;;

let expr = Addition (Multiply(Integer 2, Integer 3), Integer 1)
```

F# does not have a built-in support for evaluation of eval. However, you can use the FsLex and FsYacc from the F# PowerPack to build an abstract syntax tree parser effectively.

Summary

In this chapter, we learned about graph-related algorithms, and the implementation of our own trees. Starting from a simple binary tree, we saw several implementations of trees as well as what a balanced tree is. From there, we tackled tree searching and various traversal techniques to understand why most of the F# built-in data structures are actually based on trees.

In the next chapter, we will discuss a custom implementation of a queue. We will then introduce the FSharpX open source collection of functional data structures. Finally, we will explore the F# agent of MailboxProcessor for creating asynchronous work flows, throttling, and post-processing of results of asynchronous calls as an example usage of a queue.

Jumping the Queue

7

"A list is only as strong as its weakest link."

– Donald Knuth

"There are two ways of constructing a software design. One way is to make it so simple that there are obviously no deficiencies. And the other way is to make it so complicated that there are no obvious deficiencies."

– C.A.R. Hoare

In this chapter, we will discuss a custom functional implementation of a queue. We will then introduce the FSharpX open source collection of functional data structures. Finally, we will explore the F# agent `MailboxProcessor` for creating `async` work flows, throttling, and post-processing the results of asynchronous calls as an example usage of a queue.

In this chapter, we will cover the following topics:

- Queue data structure, typical applications using stacks
- Custom implementation versus the collection already available and the concurrent collection structures
- Using `MailboxProcessor` for throttling and scheduling a message queue

A queue is a widely used data structure that operates on the **First-In-First-Out** principle (**FIFO**). Queues can be easily implemented using a List data structure; however, the cost of accessing a list is $O(n)$ where n is the queue length. Typical variations and implementations of queues are based on their uses; for example priority queues, batch queues, and command queues are specialized queues with varying functional requirements. Queues are typically used as a fair way to regulate the waiting time for services. The key queue operations are as follows:

- Enqueue (item): Insert item at the back of the queue
- Dequeue (item): Remove (and retrieve) item from the front of the queue

As Chris Okasaki notes in his seminal writing on *Purely Functional Data Structures*, *Cambridge University Press* (June 13, 1999), fully functional queues can be implemented with two lists, front and rear. The elements are added to the rear list (the rear part of the queue), and removed from the front list (the front part of the queue). The rear elements are kept in reverse order in the rear queue, also referred to as a batched queue.

Priority queues are also another important and a frequently used variant of queues. A priority queue is an abstract data type that can hold a number of items that are accessed one-by-one, just like a queue. It differs from a queue in that the items have a *priority*. Priority queues are often implemented through heaps. In a priority queue, an element with higher priority is retrieved before an element of low priority; hence they do not operate in the strict FIFO sense of the data structure. As with the queue, enqueue(item) adds the item to the priority queue. However, the queue's dequeue(item) is internally replaced with something like RemoveMax() which returns and removes the item with the highest priority.

Microsoft .NET Framework comes with a default implementation of Queue as part of the System.Collections.Generic.Queue collection. Here is how you can instantiate and use your first simple queue implementation in F#:

```
let q = System.Collections.Generic.Queue<string>();;

q.Enqueue("1st element");;
q.Enqueue("2nd element");;
q.Enqueue("3rd element");;

q.Dequeue();;
q.Dequeue();;
q.Dequeue();;
```

Running the preceding expressions in FSI, we get the following result, as expected:

```
val it : string = "1st element"
val it : string = "2nd element"
val it : string = "3rd element"
```

Besides the generic queue, there are a few other collections in the .NET framework worth mentioning at this point, which can be easily used in F#. Like the Queue, mentioned as follows are a few other collections:

- `System.Collections.Generic.Stack<''T>`: This is a built-in stack implementation in the .NET Framework. It supports the variable-sized stack (LIFO) collection.

- `System.Collections.Generic.SortedList<''Key,''Value>`: This is a sorted collection of values represented as arrays of keys and values. The underlying search algorithm is **Binary Search**.

- `System.Collections.Generic.Dictionary<''Key,''Value>`: This is a dictionary that represents a collection of key/value pairs. Since it is implemented as a hash table, a dictionary is the fastest collection for associative key-value lookups, inserts, and deletes.

- `System.Collections.Generic.SortedDictionary<''Key,''Value>`: This is a dictionary, that is, a collection of key/value pairs sorted by the key. Similar to `SortedList`, the underlying data structure is a binary search tree.

- `System.Collections.Generic.HashSet<''T>`: This is a hash table structure for high-performance operations. This structure holds only keys and no values.

Let's make a functional queue

Following Okasaki's lead, we design our first functional queue by using two stacks. One stack will be used to to store the data, while the second stack will be used for temporary storage for the dequeue operation.

 Cornell's CS3110 Recitation 7 on Functional stacks and queues, dictionaries, fractions is an informative and recommended reading on functional data structures. For more information, go to www. cs.cornell.edu/Courses/cs3110/2011sp/recitations/ rec07.htm.

In the following algorithm, you will see this data structure unfold. Let `StackQ` be the stack in which we store the data, and let `StackTemp` be a temporary data structure.

The `Enqueue` operation is essentially just a stack push.

```
Enqueue(o):
  StackQ.push(o)
```

However, the dequeue operation requires a bit more work. While dequeueing, we pop items off the `StackQ` until we get to the bottom (first-entered) element, using `stackTemp` as a temporary store which conveniently gives back the items in the correct order for pushing back onto `StackQ` to maintain its order. We will also check the stack length for an empty stack, and pop the stack while maintaining the remainder on the `StackTemp`, as seen in the following algorithm:

```
Algorithm Dequeue():
  if StackQ is Empty then-
  Error

  deq <-StackQ.pop

  While StackQ is not empty do
    StackTemp.push(deq)
    deq <- StackQ.pop

  While StackTemp is not empty do
    temp <- StackTemp.pop
    StackQ.push(temp)
  return deq
```

This functional approach algorithm can now be easily translated to F#. Analogous to the preceding implementation, the following is the definition of a type queue with two generic stacks, a front and a rear stack. This is similar to the above implementation of `StackQ` and `StackTemp` respectively:

```
type Queue<''t>(front : stack<''t>, rear : stack<''t>) =
  let chk = function
    | EmptyStack, rear -> Queue(Stack.rev rear, EmptyStack)
    | front, rear -> Queue(front, rear)
```

The stack front stores the items in the order they are entered, and the rear stack stores the items in the reverse order. This form of storage permits the initial element in the front of the queue to be the head of the queue, as seen in the following code segment. Only selected parts of the code are provided here; for details of union types, such as StackNode and so on, please see the entire code listing provided with the book.

```
member this.hd =
  match front with
```

```
| EmptyStack -> failwith "Empty Stack"
| Node(hd, tl) -> hd
```

Consequently, the first element in the rear queue is the last item in the queue:

```
member this.tl =
  match front, rear with
  | EmptyStack, _ -> failwith "Empty Stack"
  | Node(x, f), r -> chk(front, rear)
```

For example, a queue of the alphabets `a .. f` might be represented with `f = [a;b;c]` and `r = [d;e;f]`.

To add a new item to the queue, it gets prepended to the front of the queue. This is accomplished using the `chk` method which ensures a consistent population at the front of the queue.

```
member this.enqueue(x) = chk(front, StackNode(x, rear))
```

An empty queue is essentially a queue with both empty front and rear stacks.

```
static member empty = Queue<''a>(Stack.empty, Stack.empty)
```

When there are no more items to be dequeued, a front stack will be empty. When this happens, we move all items from the rear of the queue to the front of the queue and reverse the list. In this code, you should pay special attention to the `chk` function. This function ensures that the front of the queue always has items available.

The FSharpx.Collections library

Rolling your own data structures is a profound learning experience that teaches you a great deal about the internals of storage, algorithms, and retrieval. However, it is seldom a good idea if you are writing a production code. The correctness, optimizations, testing, and continued maintenance of the built-in .NET libraries usually far outweigh the benefits gained by using a custom implementation. At this point in this book, we feel it is important to introduce a key resource, `FSharpx.Collections`. This open source library is a collection of F# data structures. These are functional implementations of various collections by community contributors. The source code for this library can be viewed, contributed to, and downloaded from `https://github.com/fsprojects/FSharpx.Collections`.

Also, the NuGet package (`https://www.nuget.org/packages/FSharpx.Collections`) can be installed through the **Package Manager Console** as shown in the following screenshot:

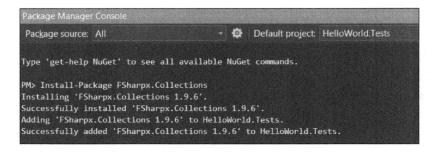

`FSharpx.Collections` contains several important and useful data structures. This includes BatchedQueue, Queue, Generic Heap, LazyList, PersistentHashMap, PersistentVector, PriorityQueue, RandomAccessList, and an immutable collection of Generic CircularBuffer, to name a few. The queue implementation in the `FSharpx.Collections` is based on a purely functional (immutable) queue, which is based on Okasaki's batched queue. The following is the introduction to a queue structure as it is created in the `FSharpx.Collections.Queue`:

Queue is an ordered linear data structure where elements are added at the end (right) and inspected and removed at the beginning (left). Ordering is by insertion history. The qualities of the Queue structure make elements first in, first out (FIFO). "head" inspects the first or left-most element in the structure, while "conj" inserts an element at the end, or right of the structure.

Further details about the Queue data structure can be seen at the respective GitHub repositories at `http://fsprojects.github.io/FSharpx.Collections/reference/fsharpx-collections-queue-1.html`) and priority queue (`http://fsprojects.github.io/FSharpx.Collections/reference/fsharpx-collections-priorityqueue.html`.

The MailboxProcessor class in F#

While we are discussing the topic of queues, it is important to note that in real-world enterprise applications, message queues are virtually everywhere. There are several sophisticated message queuing systems that provide enterprise-level queue support for high-performance applications that have robust processing, guaranteed delivery, and high-availability requirements. These applications also often use message throttling and asynchronous processing to optimize their resource needs.

In the `Microsoft.FSharp.Control` namespace, there is a `Control.MailboxProcessor<''Msg>` class that encapsulates a message queue as a light-weight agent for message processing. This `MailboxProcessor` class is defined as a message-processing agent that executes an asynchronous computation. The `MailboxProcessor` class supports one reader and multiple writing agents. It exposes methods such as `Receive`, `TryReceive`, `Scan`, and `TryScan` to wait and look for available messages. It also exposes the `CurrentQueueLength` method, which returns the number of unprocessed messages in the message queue. The benefits of using `MailboxProcessor` lies in having a dedicated and isolated message queue. This runs in its own thread with a much more light-weight implementation than actually spawning and maintaining threads. The `MailboxProcessor` class is F#'s implementation of the actor model and not a collection per se. It encapsulates a message queue, and a `MailboxProcessor` instance is called an actor or an agent (and not an async workflow) even if it does encapsulate an asynchronous computation.

Let"s explore the use of `MailboxProcessor` with a concise example. In the following code sample, we create a message type which contains an identifier and the contents of the message. We also expose a function here called `CreateMsg` that takes the contents, creates a new message object, and increases the count:

```
type Msg(msgIdentifier, msgContents) =
  static let mutable cnt = 0
  member this.ID = msgIdentifier
  member this.Contents = msgContents
  static member CreateMsg(contents) =
    cnt <- cnt + 1
    Msg(cnt, contents)
```

The `MailboxProcessor` class is a generic implementation, and here it holds a collection of `Msg`. The recursive function passed to the `MailboxProcessor` class asynchronously waits for the next message to arrive, and prints the contents when it does. In the following example, the agent's function is to print the message received. The agent here retrieves the posted message by calling the `Receive()` method. In this example, an agent monitors the queue for messages that invoke any future statements; only the message arrives in the queue:

```
let mailbox = new MailboxProcessor<Msg>(fun inbox ->
  let rec loop cnt =
    async { printfn "Msg cnt = %d. Awaiting next Msg." cnt
    let! msg = inbox.Receive()
    printfn "Msg received. ID: %d Contents: %s" msg.ID msg.Contents
    return! loop( cnt + 1) }
  loop 0)
```

Here you also see the use of the keyword `return!`. While `return` returns a result, the keyword `return!` executes an asynchronous workflow, and provides its return value as a result.

A typical syntax for the `async` operator is as follows:

```
async { expression }
```

This statement would run the expressions asynchronously, that is, without blocking the execution of other work. However, you also notice a new `let!` binding. This binding, in contrast with `let`, allows for a computation to start and then suspends the thread until the result becomes available. Once the result becomes available, it continues executing.

Here is a simple `let` expression which stores (in `res`) the results of the asynchronous operation of reading from the stream:

```
let (res : Async<byte[]>) = stream.AsyncRead(size)
```

Comparing it with `let!`, the following expression completes the `async` operation, and also returns the data:

```
let! (res : byte[])   = stream.AsyncRead(size)
```

We can now test the mailbox by creating an instance and posting some messages.

```
mailbox.Start()
mailbox.Post(Msg.CreateMsg("Knock Knock."))
mailbox.Post(Msg.CreateMsg("who's there?"))
mailbox.Post(Msg.CreateMsg("Doctor"))
mailbox.Post(Msg.CreateMsg("Doctor Who?"))
mailbox.Post(Msg.CreateMsg("Exactly"))
```

The output of the preceding invocations is processed as seen in the next screenshot, where a message is received in the `async` loop and gets printed as it arrives:

```
F# Interactive
Msg cnt = 1. Awaiting next Msg.
Msg received. ID: 2 Contents: who's there?
Msg cnt = 2. Awaiting next Msg.
Msg received. ID: 3 Contents: Doctor
Msg cnt = 3. Awaiting next Msg.
Msg received. ID: 4 Contents: Doctor Who?
Msg cnt = 4. Awaiting next Msg.
Msg received. ID: 5 Contents: Exactly
Msg cnt = 5. Awaiting next Msg.
```

Now that you understand the basic use of `MailboxProcessor`, let's improve upon the earlier example by introducing the concept of throttling. As we mentioned earlier about the built-in collections, `System.Collections.Concurrent.ConcurrentBag<T>` is a framework class library that represents a thread-safe, unordered collection of objects. In the following code example, we define a discriminated union type of message, which shows two different states: `Work` and `Quit`.

```
type Message =
    | Work
    | Quit
```

Here we also define `asyncs` as a map operation, which, as you may remember from the previous chapters, allows us to transform the elements in the input list. In this operation, we retrieve the title of the URI provided using the `url` method, and then display the longest title. The `MailboxProcessor` agent asynchronously retrieves these messages using the throttle. The complete listing is available as part of the book source code.

```
let asyncs =
urls
|> List.map (fun x -> Uri x)
|> List.map title

let throttle asyncs limit f =

let q = Queue()
let dequeue() = try q.Dequeue() |> Some with _ -> None
asyncs |> Seq.iter (fun x -> q.Enqueue x)

let agent =
MailboxProcessor.Start(fun x ->
let rec loop count =
async {
  let! msg = x.Receive()
  match msg with
  | Work ->
  let work = dequeue()
  match work with
  | Some work'' ->
  async {
    try
    do! work''
    finally
```

```
        x.Post Work
    }  |> Async.Start
    return! loop count
    | None ->
    x.Post Quit
    return! loop (count + 1)
    | Quit ->
    match count with
    | y when y = limit ->
    f |> Async.Start
    (x:> IDisposable).Dispose()
    | _ -> return! loop count
  }
  loop 0
  )
  [1 .. limit] |> List.iter (fun x -> agent.Post Work)
```

The agent, that is, the `MailboxProcessor`, contains the core of this logic. In this recursive loop, the two main conditions of the message are `Work` or `Quit`, as defined in the message type. The main `async` logic block waits for a message to be received through the `let!` statement, then looks for work in the work queue. If there is some work available, it starts the worker process: in the case of no work, it quits gracefully with `Dispose`.

Now, let's run this program with a collection of URLs:

```
let urls =
  [
  "https://www.packtpub.com/big-data-and-business-intelligence/f-
  quantitative-finance"
  "http://www.cambridge.org/us/academic/subjects/computer-science/
  programming-languages-and-applied-logic/functional-programming-
  using-f"
  ]
```

In order to maintain the concurrency of the collection, that is, programming for a situation when several streams of operations may execute concurrently against the instance, let's use `ConcurrentBag` when handling the output from the `async` operation.

```
let bag = ConcurrentBag<string>()
```

Now we will define the function `f` as the `async` operation that retrieves the longest title. This page title will be ordered by length (longest first), returned, and printed:

```
let f =
  async {
```

```
      let longestTitle = bag |> Seq.maxBy (fun x -> x.Length)
      printfn "The longest page title is: \"%s\"" longestTitle
}
```

In order to retrieve the title from the URL, we will define a function that downloads the HTML from the page, applies a simple regular expression to match the title string, and returns the title.

```
let title url =
  async {
    try
      let pattern = "(?is)<title>(.*?)</title>"
      use client = new WebClient()
      client.Encoding <- Encoding.UTF8
      let! html = client.AsyncDownloadString url
      let title =
      Regex(pattern).Match(html)
        .Groups
        .[1]
        .Value
        .Trim()
       |> WebUtility.HtmlDecode
    bag.Add title
    with
    | _ -> ()
}
```

Now, let's run our throttling function with a limit of five consecutive processes as follows:

```
throttle asyncs 5 f
```

The output of the preceding code is shown in the following screenshot:

Since our URL list is small, you won't notice the impact immediately but, as the input data set size increases, the utility of throttling becomes fairly obvious.

Summary

In this chapter, we reviewed the data structure of Queue with a custom functional implementation. We introduced the FSharpX open source collection of functional data structures. Finally, we explored the F# agent implementation of MailboxProcessor, and provided an example use of queue for creating async work flows, throttling, and post-processing.

In the next chapter, *Quick Boost with Graph*, we will briefly discuss how a graph can be functionally implemented in F#, and review the challenges associated with this task. Then we will present how to utilize QuickGraph (a standard graph library in .NET) for our purposes, explaining where to find commonly used graph implementations and discussing one of the most commonly used algorithms: Dijkstra's shortest part algorithm.

8
Quick Boost with Graph

I think of the company advertising "Thought Processors" or the college pretending that learning BASIC suffices or at least helps, whereas the teaching of BASIC should be rated as a criminal offence: it mutilates the mind beyond recovery.

– Dijkstra (1984) "The threats to computing science (EWD898)"

In the previous chapter, we reviewed the data structure of a queue; a custom implementation followed by throttling and post-processing the results of asynchronous calls as an example usage of a queue. Graphs are key data structures in computer science that represent relationships between a variety of objects (networks, circuits, Web, and relationship) using vertices and edges. In this chapter, we will briefly discuss how a graph can be implemented in a functional language, and why it is a rather difficult task to undertake. We will present a few commonly used graph implementations and discuss one of the most typical shortest-path graph implementation, Dijkstra.

In this chapter you'll learn the following topics:

- Basic graph terminology and algorithms
- Defining graphs in a functional programming setting
- Using graph data structure to implement Dijkstra's algorithm
- A primer to the graphics libraries for modeling graphs

Graphs

Graphs are one of the fundamental data structures used in computer science to represent complex structured information via a set of edges and vertices. There are several types of graphs used in algorithms including, but not limited to the following:

- **Directed graphs**: These are graphs where all edges are directed from one vertex to another
- **Undirected graphs**: These are graphs where all edges are bi-directional
- **Weighted graphs**: These are graphs with an associated label (or weight) with every edge in the graph
- **Hyper graphs**: These are graphs where one edge can connect to multiple vertices

From the computer science point of view, a graph is represented as an abstract data type that constitutes a set of finite nodes and edges.

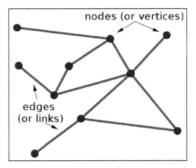

A graph data structure provides a means to represent these nodes and edges, along with some of the fundamental operations commonly used in graph algorithms. These operations include adding and removing nodes and edges, getting and setting the assigned values of the nodes (elements), and testing whether a node is an edge. Retrieving all the neighbors for a node is also one of the frequently used operations in graph algorithms.

A typical graph ADT class looks as follows:

Graph
#VertexList vertices_ #bool directed_
+Graph() +Graph(int n, bool directed) +Graph(int n) +void load(char *file) +bool directed() +int numVertices() +bool isEdge(int u, int v) +bool isEdge(int u, int v, int &weight) +int edgeWeight(int u, int v) +void addEdge(int u, int v) +void addEdge(int u, int v, int weight) +bool removeEdge(int u, int v) +VertexList :: iterator begin (int u) +VertexList :: iterator end(int u)

In a typical class diagramsuch as the one in the preceding screenshot, you see multiple constructors to create graphs with. In this example, we have methods like load that may take the input of a file which contains a graph definition, and create a graph using this data. The flag directed defines whether the graph is directed, and can be get/set upon the construction of the graph. The operations allow us to add and remove edges, and determine the number of vertices.

As we read in *Chapter 6*, *See the Forest for the Trees*, the tree is also a special case of a graph. Specifically, it is an undirected graph where any two nodes are connected by exactly one edge. Now let's proceed to see how we can model graphs using F#.

Modeling graphs using F#

A graph can be modelled in multiple ways. For instance, we can simply represent it as a collection of vertices and edges. Alternatively, it can be defined as a set of tuples containing a vertex and a set of corresponding edges. In either approach, we have to consider space-time trade-off. For example, in order to effectively represent a graph where paths can be determined quickly, we can build a data structure, which encapsulates the set of vertices and edges. However, this will result in an exponential growth of the space proportional to the square of the number of vertices.

Now, we will show one approach to model a graph in F#. The individual constructs defined here, as well as the complete code listing, can be found in the source code of the book at http://www.packtpub.com/support. In our representation, a graph consists of nodes and edges, as shown in the following code snippet:

```
type Graph() =
   let mutable nodes = []
   let mutable edges = []
   member this.Nodes with get() = nodes
   member this.Edges with get() = edges
```

In the preceding code, you see the use of the `with` keyword. It is a versatile keyword used in various contexts such as in match expressions, object expressions, type extensions, and in the context of exception handling, that is, the `try...with` expressions. In this context, we are using `get` as a part of the object expression that allows us to avoid the extra code and overhead that is required to create a new, named type. For a detailed discussion on the keyword within different contexts, please refer to the F# keyword reference.

In order to add a new node, we create a member of type graph that applies a match expression. This expression searches for the node with a union type (`Some`, `None`) which checks if a node already exists in the collection with ID provided as a parameter. If the node doesn't exist, it creates the node with the given ID.

```
member this.CreateNode(id) =
   match this.FindNode id with
     | Some(n) -> None
     | None ->    i
       let node = Node(this, ID=id)
       nodes <- nodes @ [ node ]
     Some node
```

Every node has an associated ID element used as an identifier. To create an edge from the node, we apply similar logic; first find the `from` node, directing to the `to` node and see if there exists an edge. If it doesn't, we create an edge and add it to the edge collection. Here you will see the use of `` `...` `` operator that is quite interesting and handy. Since `to` is used in for loops to indicate a range, the `` `...` `` operator delimits the identifier "to", which otherwise, being a reserved keyword, would not be a legal identifier:

```
member this.CreateEdgeFromNode(from:Node, ``to``:Node, id) =
   match this.FindEdge id with
   | Some(edge) -> None
```

```
  | None ->
    let edge = Edge(this, from, ``to``, ID=id)
    from.AddOutgoingEdge(edge)
    ``to``.AddIncomingEdge(edge)
    edges <- edges @ [edge]
    Some edge
```

Last but not the least, to find the node and edges, we iterate through the sequence using the `Seq.tryFind<'T>` function of the sequence. The function finds an element that satisfies the specified predicate.

```
Seq.tryFind : ('T -> bool) -> seq<'T> -> 'T option
```

The `member` methods for finding the node and edges, use the predicate to look up the node based on the ID.

```
member this.FindNode(id) =
  (nodes:Node list) |> Seq.tryFind(fun n -> n.ID = id)
  member this.FindEdge(id) =
    (edges:Edge list) |> Seq.tryFind(fun edge -> edge.ID = id)
```

Based on these fundamental constructs, we have specified here how the graph can be represented. The complete listing of the graph data structure can be found in the source code of the book at http://www.packtpub.com/support.

Let's solve some problems involving graphs to understand the concepts and implementation in practice.

The shortest path algorithm

Finding the shortest path, and optimization of routes based on time and distance, has countless implementations in the real world for transportation and map-related applications. The same algorithms also apply to network routing protocols such as **Intermediate System to Intermediate System (IS-IS)** and **OSPF (Open Shortest Path First)**. There are various algorithms, optimizations, and heuristics available to solve shortest path problems including, but not limited to, A*, Dijkstra, and the Bellman-Ford algorithm.

In graph theory, Dijkstra's shortest-path algorithm is one of the most well-known algorithms. It is a special case of the A* algorithm, which helps in solving the problem of finding the shortest path in a graph, from the source node to the destination. This problem is also known as a single-source shortest path problem because it is possible to discover the shortest path given the single source (vertex).

In various practical applications, each link or edge of the graph bears an associated numerical value called **weight**. The weight represents the cost of the edge, for instance, measuring the length of the route taken, or the time taken to travel a route and so on. The Bellman-Ford algorithm can be applied if the weights are negative.

The more general A* (A-star) algorithm adds heuristic intelligence to guide its search path instead of indiscriminately following fixed strategies. The iteratively ordered search algorithm shown next keeps a set of open states to explore in order to reach the goal state. The algorithm steps are given as follows:

1. Start by adding the starting node to the open collection.
2. Repeat the following:

    1. Calculate the *Cost f(x)=g(x)+h(x)* where:

3. *g* is the cost of moving from the starting node A to another node, following the path generated to get there.
4. *h* is the heuristic, that is, the estimated (guess) movement cost to move from the current node to the destination node. The heuristic *h(x)* cost must be strictly optimistic.

    1. Search for the lowest *f* cost node in the open list (current node).
    2. Move it to the closed collection.
    3. For each of the nodes adjacent to this current node,

5. If the node is unreachable, ignore the node:
6. If the node is on the closed collection, ignore the node.
7. If the node is not on the open collection, add it to the open collection. Also, make the current node the parent of this node. Calculate the f, g, and *h* costs of the path traversed.
8. If the node is part of the open collection, use *g*'s cost to measure the best path to the destination node. Sort the open list by the *f* score. Substitute the parent of the node with the least cost, with the current node.

    1. Terminate when:

9. You find the destination node as part of the closed collection.
10. You find that the open collection is empty, that is, there is no path to reach the destination.

Now, if you save the traversed path, and work backwards from the destination to the source node, you will discover it to be the shortest path. Due to its *admissible heuristic* nature, the A* search only traverses a promising node by focusing on reaching the destination. If your heuristic function is efficient in evaluating the potential costs, fewer nodes get traversed. The heuristics make it more efficient and fun, however it is beyond the scope of this text.

Similar to A*, in Dijkstra's algorithm, for a given node in the graph, the algorithm discovers the path with the smallest weight, which is usually the shortest path. The algorithm can be terminated once the shortest path between the source and destination has been determined. Dijkstra is a special case for A* when the heuristics (H) is zero.

The algorithm, as defined by Dasgupta in *Algorithms*, can be seen in the following figure:

```
ALGORITHM   Dijkstra(G, s)
    //Dijkstra's algorithm for single-source shortest paths
    //Input: A weighted connected graph G = ⟨V, E⟩ with nonnegative weights
    //        and its vertex s
    //Output: The length dᵥ of a shortest path from s to v
    //         and its penultimate vertex pᵥ for every vertex v in V
    Initialize(Q)  //initialize vertex priority queue to empty
    for every vertex v in V do
        dᵥ ← ∞;  pᵥ ← null
        Insert(Q, v, dᵥ)  //initialize vertex priority in the priority queue
    dₛ ← 0;  Decrease(Q, s, dₛ)  //update priority of s with dₛ
    V_T ← Ø
    for i ← 0 to |V| − 1 do
        u* ← DeleteMin(Q)  //delete the minimum priority element
        V_T ← V_T ∪ {u*}
        for every vertex u in V − V_T that is adjacent to u* do
            if d_{u*} + w(u*, u) < d_u
                d_u ← d_{u*} + w(u*, u);  p_u ← u*
                Decrease(Q, u, d_u)
```

In the preceding algorithm, we take inputs in the form of Graph G, the edge lengths, and the vertex s to find the shortest path. The output is the set of distances to all the vertices reachable from s. The `Makequeue` method builds a queue out of the given elements, with the given key values. The `decreasekey` function allows for a decrement in the key value of a particular element while `deletemin` returns the element with the smallest key, and removes it from the set.

To understand this algorithm in a more concrete manner, let's implement Dijkstra's algorithm in F#. We start doing this by solving one of the Project Euler problems, which is a restricted version of Dijkstra's generic case. The problem statement in **Euler #81** states the following:

 In the 5 x 5 matrix displayed in the following figure, the minimal path sum from the top left to the bottom right, by only moving to the right and down, is indicated in bold red and is equal to 2427.

$$\begin{pmatrix} 131 & 673 & 234 & 103 & 18 \\ 201 & 96 & 342 & 965 & 150 \\ 630 & 803 & 746 & 422 & 111 \\ 537 & 699 & 497 & 121 & 956 \\ 805 & 732 & 524 & 37 & 331 \end{pmatrix}$$

Finding the minimal path sum

The problem provides an 80 x 80 matrix in a text file, allowing traversal from the top left to the bottom right by only moving right and down.

As we discussed above, Dijkstra has one cost function which helps to find the shortest path from the source node to every other node by considering only the real cost (in contrast with A* heuristic). In order to solve the matrix problem, let's see how the graph implementation helps us.

First of all we will iterate through the matrix file and read the comma-delimited costs in the array. You can see the implementation in the following code snippet:

```
let weights = File.ReadAllLines("matrix.txt")
   |> Array.map(fun line -> line.Split(',') |> Array.map int32)
let matrixHeight = weights.Length;
let matrixWidth = weights.[0].Length;
```

As in the graph type described above, let's declare a node. A node consists of a list of coordinates (2D) for the matrix coordinates and the parent node, as well as the cost (weight).

```
type Node = {
  Coordinates: int*int
  mutable Parent: Node
  mutable Weight: int
  }
```

Now to the cost function; the cost of traversing to a node is the sum of two entities: the cost of moving to its parent and the original cost provided. The following is the code to calculate the cost:

```
let cost sourceNode (x, y) =
  sourceNode.Weight + weights.[y].[x]
```

Let's define the vicinity function that will provide all the nodes in the vicinity of the current node. Since the premise of this problem limits the movement to down and right, it is fairly easy to calculate by increasing the x and y coordinates. Since there are no diagonals, we cannot simultaneously increase these values.

```
let vicinity node =
  let coords = function
    | x, y when (x < matrixWidth - 1 && y < matrixHeight - 1) -> [(x +
1, y); (x, y + 1)]
    | x, y when (x < matrixWidth - 1) -> [(x + 1, y)]
    | x, y when (y < matrixHeight - 1) -> [(x, y + 1)]
    | _ -> []
  coords(node.Coordinates) |> List.map (fun coord -> { node with
Coordinates = coord;
    Parent = node;
    Weight = cost node coord })
```

We now need to initialize our matrix (top left) and the open and closed collections as defined in the algorithm.

```
let rec startNode = { Coordinates = 0, 0; Parent = startNode; Weight =
weights.[0].[0] }

let rec endNode = { Coordinates = matrixWidth - 1, matrixHeight - 1;
Parent = endNode; Weight = Int32.MaxValue }

let currentNode = startNode

let openCollection = new ResizeArray<Node>()
let closedCollection = new ResizeArray<Node>()
```

Another helpful function is to validate whether the node exists in the given set. This will help us validate the node's existence in a collection.

```
let existsIn set node =
  set |> Seq.exists(fun n -> n.Coordinates = node.Coordinates)
```

With initializations and helper methods out of the way, let's focus on the main algorithm. The `PathFinder` method iterates through the nodes applying Dijkstra's algorithm and returns the path (set of nodes).

The algorithm begins with initializing the open collection with the starting node.

```
let PathFinder () =
  openCollection.Add(startNode)
```

It needs to iterate through until the closed collection does not contain the terminating node.

```
while not(endNode |> existsIn closedCollection) do
```

Let's find the node with the minimum weight in the open collection. This will be our current node.

```
let currentNode = openCollection |> Seq.minBy (fun node -> node.
Weight)
```

Now move this node to the closed collection.

```
openCollection.RemoveAll(fun node -> node.Coordinates = currentNode.
Coordinates) |> ignore
closedCollection.Add(currentNode)
```

While iterating through the vicinity nodes, we ignore a node if it cannot be traversed (unreachable), or is in the closed collection.

```
let vicinityNodes = vicinity currentNode |> List.filter ((existsIn
closedCollection) >> not)
for node in vicinityNodes do
```

If the node is not a part of the open collection, make the current node the parent of this node and calculate the cost of the node:

```
match openCollection |> Seq.tryFind (fun n -> n.Coordinates = node.
Coordinates) with
  | None -> (openCollection.Add(node)
    node.Parent <- currentNode
    node.Weight <- cost currentNode node.Coordinates)
```

If the open collection does not have this node, we try to determine if the current path to the node is a better path in terms of weight, using the lower value of G. As seen in the union below, if it is the minimum path, we change the parent of the node to the current node and re-evaluate the cost function.

```
| Some(n) -> (let newCost = cost currentNode n.Coordinates
   if newCost < n.Weight then
     n.Parent <- currentNode
     n.Weight <- newCost)
```

The resulting path is determined with recursive back tracking.

```
let rec walkBack node =
  seq {
    if node.Coordinates <> startNode.Coordinates then
      yield! walkBack node.Parent
    yield node
  }
walkBack (closedCollection.Find(fun n -> n.Coordinates = endNode.
Coordinates))
```

We invoke the main function, which returns us the path and the corresponding weights.

```
do
  let path = PathFinder()
  for n in path do
    let x, y = n.Coordinates
    printfn "%A %A" n.Coordinates weights.[y].[x]
  printfn "Weights of the traversed path: %A" (Seq.last path).Weight
```

In order to render and display charts and graphs using F#, we have a few options at our disposal, listed as follows:

- Graph# (http://graphsharp.codeplex.com/) uses QuickGraph as a data structure/algorithm library at http://quickgraph.codeplex.com/

- For more information on **Direct Graph Markup Language (DGML)** refer to Skinner's blog at, http://blogs.msdn.com/b/camerons/archive/2009/01/26/directed-graph-markup-language-dgml.aspx=

- For more information on **F# Charting: Library for Data Visualization**, (charts and graphs), refer to fsharp.github.io/FSharp.Charting/

Summary

In this chapter, we briefly reviewed graphs and the related algorithms, starting with basic graph terminology and delved into the representation of graphs in a functional programming setting. We then implemented Dijkstra's algorithm to a Project Euler problem, and listed a few graphics libraries for modeling graphs.

In the next chapter, we are going to discuss set, map, and vectors. We will tackle a custom implementation of a vector, including several optimizations. Additionally, we will review the .NET's intermediate language and see how the code translates in a multi-language scenario. This includes F# IL generation and comparing it with C# IL to demonstrate how the intermediate language provides the very foundation of execution in the .NET Framework-based applications.

9

Sets, Maps, and Vectors of Indirections

"All problems in computer science can be solved by another level of indirection, except of course for the problem of too many indirections."

– David Wheeler

"A language that doesn't affect the way you think about programming is not worth knowing."

– Alan J. Perlis

In the last chapter, we reviewed graphs and the related algorithms, starting with basic graph terminology and delved into how to represent graphs in a functional programming setting. We then used the graph data structure to implement Dijkstra's algorithm and provided a brief primer to the graphics libraries for modeling graphs.

In this chapter, we are going to review **sets** and **maps**, and will explore a custom implementation of a **vector**. Additionally, we are going to discuss intermediate language and how it works in the .NET ecosystem. We will also cover F# IL generation and compare it with C#.

In this chapter, we will cover the following topics:

- Sets and maps
- Vectors and cross-pollination of ideas (from Conjure and Scala to F#)
- **Intermediate Language** (IL) in the .NET ecosystem
- F#, C#, and the generation of the IL code

Sets and maps

We discussed sets and maps briefly during the F# primer. Sets are standard data structures in most functional languages. In F#, these key data structures are also supported along with lists and sequences, and are implemented as immutable AVL trees. An AVL tree, named for G. **A**delson-**V**elsky and E. M. **L**andis, is a self-balancing binary search tree that is an efficient data structure. AVL trees support insertion, deletion, and search operations in $O(log\ n)$ time where n is the number of nodes (elements). Nodes are often referred to as elements as they are used to store the values (elements) in the tree.

A set collection is a container for unique items as it does not allow duplicates. Sets do not preserve the order in which the elements are inserted. Following is an example of Set:

```
Set.empty.Add(3).Add(2).Add(7);;
val it : Set<int> = set [1; 2; 7]
```

Another data structure implementation, similar to sets, is **map**. A map is basically a dictionary, that is, a special kind of set which associates keys with values. The Collections.Map<'Key, 'Value> class provides support for the immutable key value pairs (maps) where keys are ordered by the F# generic comparison. The Map implementation is thread-safe and is suitable for concurrent use from multi-threaded applications. The source code for maps can be found at (FSharp.Core\map.fs) within the listing in the GitHub repository https://github.com/Microsoft/visualfsharp/blob/fsharp4/src/fsharp/FSharp.Core/map.fs.

The following is an example of a map:

```
let bibTeXBiblio = Map.empty.Add("agrawal1996fast", "Fast Discovery of
Association Rules.")
.Add("bell2009beyond", "Beyond the data deluge")
.Add("Wooldridge2003", "Bayesian Belief Networks")
.Add("Witten2005", "Data Mining: Practical machine learning tools and
techniques");;
```

And the elements can be accessed similar to arrays as follows:

```
bibTeXBiblio.["Wooldridge2003"]
```

The reason behind revisiting sets and maps here is to look at the implementations of these popular data structures, and learn from them. Like most programming concepts, you need to really understand the fundamentals before looking into advanced materials. A brief review of the implementation of these fundamental data structures opens a window to understand the design considerations and the respective trade-offs. For instance, you realize that an immutable data structure, once a set's node is created, cannot be changed. Also as an immutable structure, if we perform n insertions, you end up with the $n+1$ versions of the tree.

In order to view the F# set and map (virtually any collection), you can download the entire source from the F# GitHub repository at `https://github.com/Microsoft/visualfsharp`. The source code for the set-related operations can be found at `fsharp-master\fsharp-master\src\fsharp\FSharp.Core\Set.fs`.

In about a thousand lines of code for Microsoft FSharp's built-in `Set.fs` implementation, you will see the `SetTree<'T>` type, the `Set` module, and the `SetTree` modules. In the code segment given next, you will notice that `SetTree` is a type constructor where the parameter it takes is a comparable type `'T`, with `:` type annotation. The `:` separates a parameter or member identifier from its type. The type definition provides the union type for a set of nodes and the corresponding iterator information. Refer to the following code:

```
type SetTree<'T> when 'T : comparison =
    | SetEmpty
    | SetNode of 'T * SetTree<'T> *  SetTree<'T> * int
    | SetOne  of 'T
module internal SetTree =
    type SetIterator<'T> when 'T : comparison  =
      { mutable stack: SetTree<'T> list;
        mutable started : bool
      }
```

The equality and comparison constraints, `type : equality` and `type : comparison` respectively, are new and first-class primary constraints in the F# language. As the name suggests, the comparison type definition implies that a type must implement the `System.IComparable` namespace.

You also see the use of the keyword module in the preceding code with the access control qualifier (internal). A local module declaration follows:

```
module [accessibility-modifier] module-name =
    declarations
```

The preceding example is of a nested module. A module helps to group the F# code constructs such as types, values, function values, and code and we use it here to define the `SetIterator`. Similarly, following are the corresponding `SetIterator<'T>` types and related functions which are used for implementing the `IEnumerable` interface:

```
type Set<'T when 'T : comparison >(comparer:IComparer<'T>, tree:
SetTree<'T>) =
  //member functions:
  //  Add, Remove, Contains, etc.
  //operators:
  //  - + Intersection, etc.
  //overrides:
  //  GetHashCode, Equals, ToString
  //implement interfaces:
  //  IComparable
  //  ICollection<'T>
  //  IEnumerable<'T>
  //  IEnumerable
module Set =
    // set module functions:
    // add, isEmpty, etc.
```

The underlying implementation of this data structure, that is, the AVL tree rebalancing using rotations, is an interesting algorithm to study. An AVL tree distinguishes itself from a binary search tree as its balance factor gets calculated for every node. The balance factor for a node, is the difference between the height of the left subtree and the height of the right subtree. Also, the AVL tree design dictates that for every node, the height of the left and right subtrees can differ by no more than 1. Therefore, if the insert causes the balance factor to become 2 or -2 for the newly inserted node, it requires an adjustment of the tree by rotation around the node.

A simple AVL tree can be defined as follows:

```
type 't AvlTree =
  member Height : int
  member Left : 't AvlTree
  member Right : 't AvlTree
  member Value : 't
  member Insert : 't -> 't AvlTree
  member Contains : 't -> bool
```

Tree rotation, that is, moving one node up and the other node down in the tree, is a fairly common operation used to change the shape of the tree, that is, to decrease the height of the tree by moving smaller subtrees down and larger subtrees up. The structure changes do not interfere with the order of the elements.

> *The AVL Tree Rotations Tutorial* by John Hargrove can be found
> at http://pages.cs.wisc.edu/~paton/readings/
> liblitVersion/AVL-Tree-Rotations.pdf.

AVL trees are efficient data structures that are always balanced, and hence provide the search complexity of $(log\ n)$. Consequently, insertions and deletions are also $O(logn)$. Since AVL trees balance their heights constantly, this allows for the speed of insertion to be consistent by a constant factor. Since *log n* is roughly the height of the tree, which is the length of the longest search path from the root to any node in the tree. In other words, the path from the root of the tree has the length of *O(log N)*, therefore the total time taken for adjusting the node is *O(log N)*. Along with its many merits, one deterrent in using AVL trees is that they are more complicated to program and debug. They also require more space for balancing, which takes time.

Vectors

Lists are an effective data structure when the processing is focused mainly on the head element, which takes a constant time to access. For the elements further within the list, the access time is linearly proportional to the depth of the list, that is, their position within the list. This random access issue on the list is addressed by vectors in various functional (or multi-paradigm) programming languages such as Scala. Scala is to JVM what F# is to .NET. A vector is built as a collection type based on bit-mapped vector tries, providing a solution to the inadequacy of random access on lists.

> A discussion on bit vector optimization and tries are beyond the scope
> of this book. However, you can find an excellent talk on *Persistent
> Data Structures and Managed References* by Rich Hickey, the author of
> Clojure at www.infoq.com/presentations/Value-Identity-
> State-Rich-Hickey.

The conventional implementation of vectors can rapidly access an indexed array element. However, a bitmapped vector tree is faster in operations such as creating a new copy with a single changed element, without affecting the original data structure.

Vectors are implemented as an immutable data structure for random access and updates in constant time. They are completely different from the vectors in mathematics, which can be represented by a custom type containing magnitude and direction. To elaborate, it is not the following vector:

> *Vector: "I'm applying for a villain loan. I go by the name of Vector. It's a mathematical term, represented by an arrow with both direction and magnitude. Vector! That's me, because I commit crimes with both direction and magnitude. Oh yeah!"*

> *– Despicable Me.*

Since in F# there is no default implementation of Vector, the FSharpX collection provides one as a part of `FSharpx.Collections`, which defines it as follows:

`PersistentVector` is an ordered linear structure implementing the inverse of the List signature, (last, initial, conj) in place of (head, tail, cons). Indexed lookup or update (returning a new immutable instance of vector) of any element is $O\ log\ (n)$ Length is $O\ (1)$ where, ordering is by insertion history.

The following selected class definition of `PersistentVector` gives insight into available functionality and the members. A `PersistentVector` is implemented as a collection of values indexed by contiguous integers. As the API documentation describes, it supports access to items by an index in $log\ (n)$ hops. The persistent vectors are immutable, therefore a new version can be created without destroying the old copy.

`FSharpx.Collections` is a collection of data structures used with F# and C#. The project can be installed via NuGet Package Manager and can be downloaded from `http://fsprojects.github.io/FSharpx.Collections/index.html`:

```
type PersistentVector<'T> =
  interface System.Collections.Generic.IEnumerable<'T>
  interface System.Collections.IEnumerable
  /// O(1). Returns a new vector with the element added at the end.
  member Conj : 'T -> PersistentVector<'T>
  /// O(n). Returns a new vector without the last item. If the
collection is empty it throws an exception.
```

```
member Initial : PersistentVector<'T>


/// O(n). Returns option vector without the last item.
member TryInitial : PersistentVector<'T> option
/// O(log32n). Returns vector element at the index.
member Item : int -> 'T with get
/// O(1). Returns the last element in the vector. If the vector is
empty it throws an exception.
member Last : 'T


/// O(1). Returns option last element in the vector.
member TryLast : 'T option


/// O(1). Returns the number of items in the vector.
member Length : int


///O(n). Returns random access list reversed.
member Rev : unit -> PersistentVector<'T>


/// O(1). Returns tuple last element and vector without last item
member Unconj : PersistentVector<'T> * 'T


/// O(log32n). Returns a new vector that contains the given value at
the index.
member Update : int * 'T -> PersistentVector<'T>


/// O(log32n). Returns option vector that contains the given value
at the index.
member TryUpdate : int * 'T -> PersistentVector<'T> option
```

 The entire source code is also available at https://github.com/
fsprojects/FSharpx.Collections/blob/master/src/
FSharpx.Collections/PersistentVector.fs.

This implementation of a persistent vector can be used for various general-purpose tasks as you have seen earlier. You can use persistent vectors to convert a sequence of values as follows:

```
let seqVector = ofSeq [1..10]
val intVector : FSharpx.Collections.PersistentVector<int>
```

You can also square all values in a `PersistentVector` as shown in the following code snippet:

```
let squareVector' = map (fun x -> x * x) seqVector
intVector'.[3]
val it : int = 256
```

Functional programing languages liberally take inspiration from each other regarding the implementation of data structures and algorithms. **Clojure**, a popular functional programming language, is a dialect of Lisp and provides a rich set of immutable, persistent data structures. The FSharpX vector implementation is actually ported from Clojure. For more information on Clojure, refer to `https://github.com/clojure/clojure/blob/master/src/jvm/clojure/lang/Vector.java`.

The data structures discussed earlier are quite popular in the functional community since they are immutable and readable. They also support value equality semantics and the corresponding hash values. Almost all functional data structures ideally possess the attributes specified previously; in addition, these collections should also support modern programming language features such as iteratibility, manipulability through interfaces, sequencing, and type casting.

No book on functional programming is complete without mentioning **Zipper** — a purely functional data structure for manipulating immutable data structures originally created by Gerard Huet and published in the Journal of functional programming. A zipper data structure is rather remarkably ingenious even though it is not really just a single data structure. Instead, zipper is a way of building data structures in functional languages to provide a degree of parity with the mutability of imperative languages, by implementing the idea of focal points for edits. By default, functional programming languages such as Haskell and Clojure provide the implementation of Zipper but F# does not have one as a part of its built-in library. You can find the FSharpX implementation at `FSharpx.Collections/src/FSharpx.Collections.Experimental/ListZipper.fs`.

Functional Pearl – the Zipper by Gerard Huet can be found at `https://www.st.cs.uni-saarland.de/edu/seminare/2005/advanced-fp/docs/huet-zipper.pdf`.

F# and the Intermediate Language

CIL (**Common Intermediate Language**), **MSIL** (**Microsoft Intermediate Language**), or **IL**, is the intermediate representation of the higher level .NET languages. As a part of the **CLI** (**Common Language Infrastructure**), IL serves as a human-readable intermediate language that is shared by all high-level .NET languages and is generated prior to the static or dynamic compilation of the machine-specific code.

CIL and MSIL are effectively synonymous and there isn't much difference between the two. CIL is the terminology used in the CLI standard while MSIL is the product term for Microsoft's implementation of the standard. Both apply to the CPU-independent instruction set. The CLR executes after a high-level language such as F#, C#, VB, C++, Python, Ruby, and so on has compiled.

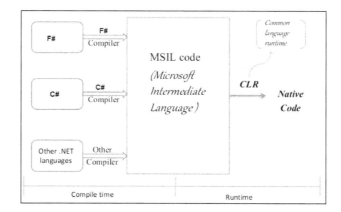

F# belongs to the family of the .NET IL languages such as C# and VB.NET. The compilers for these languages output IL; **JIT** (**Just-In-Time**) compilation converts the IL to native code on demand, at runtime. Since JIT operates on demand, that is, converts an assembly's MSIL to native code only when a function is called, this leads to performance issues at runtime. **Microsoft NGEN** (**CLR Native Image Generator**) provides the optimization which creates native images (files containing compiled processor-specific machine code), and uses them as a part of the native image cache. Therefore, runtime uses these images for execution instead of using the JIT compiler to compile the original assembly.

You can see the process flow in the diagram that follows:

This intermediate language may sound like an extra step; why go through one more stage instead of just generating the machine code as in the good old days? The reality is, this approach has allowed the development of multiple higher-level languages and DSL (**Domain Specific Languages**) on both JVM and .NET. Functional languages in .NET are largely available today due to the CLR interoperability. The cross-platform advantage of running the same program on multiple platforms such as Windows, Linux, and MacOS (through Mono), is a significant advantage. Having the same output executed via the CLR makes it possible to mix and match multiple IL-based languages in a simple application. It also allows libraries from different languages to be used across applications, hence increasing the reusability.

In order to generate the IL corresponding to the code, you need to compile your F# project to a .dll file. For instance, in the following screenshot we get ILDemo.dll provided as a part of the accompanying source code:

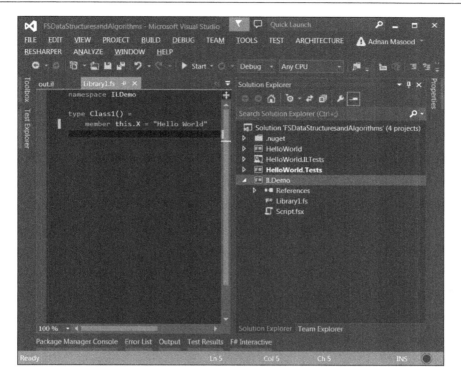

Now you can use **ILDASM** (**IL disassembler**) on the DLL file to see the information about the DLL, as seen in the following screenshot:

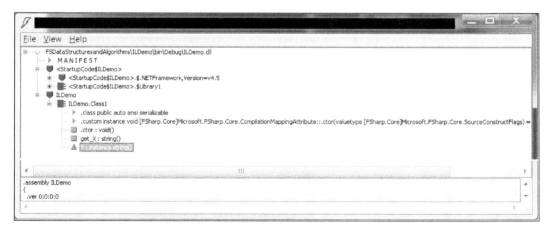

For more information on ILDASM, refer to
https://msdn.microsoft.com/en-us/
library/f7dy01k1%28v=vs.110%29.aspx.

You can also start it by typing `ildasm` from the **Developer Command Prompt** for
VS 2013 which can be started by going to **Start | All Programs | Microsoft Visual
Studio 2013 | Visual Studio Tools | Developer Command Prompt**.

Now, you can generate the IL code by using the dump option from the **FILE** menu.
The IL code looks as seen in the following screenshot:

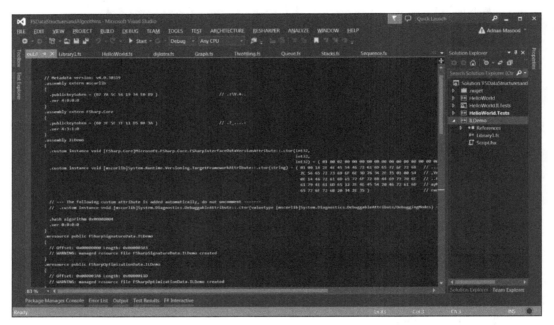

Partial IL listing for the simple 'hello world' program can be seen as follows:

```
.method public hidebysig specialname instance string
  get_X() cil managed
  {
    // Code size       7 (0x7)
    .maxstack  8
    IL_0000:  nop
    IL_0001:  ldstr      "Hello World"
    IL_0006:  ret
  }
// end of method Class1::get_X
```

Here you can see the load string IL method, which has the `Hello World` string in there. A similar C# code for the following property is:

```
public class Class1
{
  public string X
  {
    get { return X; }
    set { X = "Hello World"; }
  }
}
```

This results in a very similar IL:

```
.method public hidebysig specialname instance void set_X(string
'value') cil managed
{
  // Code size       14 (0xe)
  .maxstack  8
  IL_0000:  nop
  IL_0001:  ldarg.0
  IL_0002:  ldstr      "Hello World"
  IL_0007:  call       instance void ILDemoCS.Class1::set_X(string)
  IL_000c:  nop
  IL_000d:  ret
}
// end of method Class1::set_X
```

This congruency for different languages in the IL code explains the portability of shared libraries. Although different high-level languages such as C#, VB.NET, F#, Iron Python and so on vary in syntax, they all compile to IL, which allows them to able to share codebase and functionality among each other.

Microsoft has recently developed a .NET Compiler Platform (dubbed Project Roslyn) that exposes the internal components through the API's. The platform constitutes of **Compiler APIs**, **Services APIs**, and **Editor Services APIs** in order to support granular control over compilation. This approach of exposing the compiler as a service is currently being supported only for C#.NET and VB.NET leaving F# behind, which hinders many opportunities for innovation, including meta-programming, code generation, and transformation. As a reprieve, F# compiler services are available at `http://fsharp.github.io/FSharp.Compiler.Service/`; these are not nearly as good as Roslyn, but make it possible to build stuff like Visual F# Power Tools, FSharp.Formatting, and more.

Summary

In this chapter, we reviewed sets and maps, and explored an implementation of the vector data type. Additionally, we viewed some .NET intermediate languages and saw the translated IL code in the multi-language scenario. We have also covered F# IL generation and compared it with C# IL to demonstrate how the intermediate language provides the very foundation of execution in the .NET framework-based applications. Regardless of what language you write the code in, it eventually gets translated to intermediate language as the lowest common denominator.

In the next and final chapter, we suggest other resources from which the reader can learn much more. We start with referencing the F# source code itself, pointing to data structures in the code. We will walk shortly over the FSharpX and Deedle custom implementations, enlisting extended data structures and alternatives.

The final chapter includes obligatory references to the seminal work in this field. This includes *Purely Functional Data Structures* by Okasaki, *Pearls of Functional Algorithm Design* by Richard Bird, and several other important academic resources. Finally, we point to Haskell, OCaml, Clojure, and Scala for inspiration when looking for solutions to common problems encountered by functional programmers.

10
Where to Go Next?

"It is my firm belief that all successful languages are grown and not merely designed from first principles."

– *Bjarne Stroustrup*

This book intends to provide a practical introduction to the vast subject matter area of F# data structures and functional programming. In this short text, we have barely been able to explore the metaphorical tip of the functional-programming-with-F# iceberg. We would like to suggest other resources from which the reader can learn much more. Following is the detailed list of different resources around the functional ecosystem, and the F# programming language. In the references below, you would see various guides, source codes, and links which will assist you in getting further information.

In this chapter, we will cover the following topics:

- References and further readings
- F# language resources
- Component design guides
- Functional programming guides
- Books and interactive tutorials
- Video tutorials
- Community projects
- General Functional programming
- Academic resources

References and further readings

As an aspiring or a seasoned F# developer looking for F# resources, the **F# Software Foundation** (http://fsharp.org/) should be your first stop. The F# Software foundation website is a one-stop shop for language documentation, reference, and specification.

Don Syme's blog, who's the designer and architect of the F# language (http://blogs.msdn.com/dsyme) and his Twitter feeds (https://twitter.com/dsyme) are excellent resources to keep up with the state of F#. If you like to see sample code and tweak it to learn, the MSDN F# Code Samples (https://code.msdn.microsoft.com/ and check the F# box under **Programming language**) should be among your list of favorites/bookmarks.

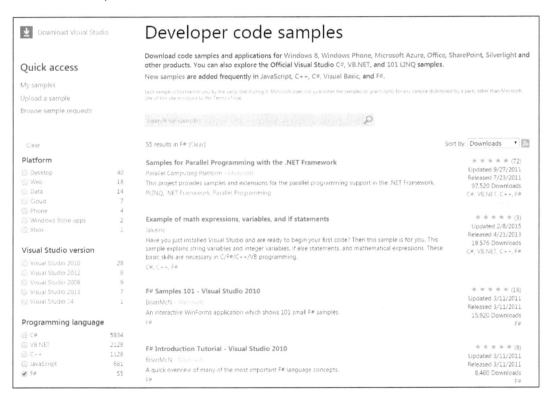

If you wish to possess more information on functional data structures, the most famous and widely acclaimed work on purely functional data structures comes from Chris Okasaki's dissertation, *Purely Functional Data Structures*. This dissertation is also available as a book, which depicts Okasaki's research work on the systematic exploration of implementing advanced data structures in a purely functional way. Okasaki's dissertation is available through the Carnegie Mellon website at `http://www.cs.cmu.edu/~rwh/theses/okasaki.pdf`.

Please refer to the *Academic resources* section in this chapter for further details.

F# language resources

The F# Software Foundation website and MSDN provide a substantial amount of F# resources. This includes language documentation, programming resources, code samples, general information about F# programming, language adaption tips and tricks, community contributions, programming language reference, and standard F# library documentation.

- **F# Language Reference**: This resource provides reference information about the F# language, including information about keywords, symbols, and operators. This is available at `http://msdn.microsoft.com/en-us/library/dd233181.aspx`.

- **F# Core Library Reference**: This source provides reference information about the F# core library, `FSharp.Core.dll` and is available at `http://msdn.microsoft.com/en-us/library/ee353567.aspx`.

- **F# Type Providers**: This resource introduces information-rich programming features available in F# 3.0 to explain how to consume external data sources such as SQL, web services, and so on, at `http://msdn.microsoft.com/en-us/library/hh156509.aspx`.

- **Real-World Functional Programming (MSDN Blog)**: This is the selection of chapters from the book by the same title, written by Tomas Petricek, Jon Skeet, and Yin Zhu. This book introduces functional programming in F#, server-side and client-side application development, data visualization and numerical computing `http://msdn.microsoft.com/en-us/library/hh314518`.

- **The F# Language Specification**: The language specification provides an exhaustive technical description of the programming language and the underlying facets of the intermediate language. The specifications are especially interesting for those already familiar with the functional programming paradigm and looking to explore the F# language constructs and expected compiler actions. The language specification outlines the version changes, lexical analysis, language grammar, pattern matching, type inference algorithm, and so on, at `http://fsharp.org/specs/language-spec`.

- The F# 2.0 Language Specification can be found at http://www.scribd.com/doc/40950295/FSharp-Language-Specification-2-0
- The F# 3.0 Language Specification can be found at http://fsharp.org/specs/language-spec/3.0/FSharpSpec-3.0-final.pdf
- The F# 3.1 Language Specification (working draft) can be found at http://fsharp.org/specs/language-spec/3.1/FSharpSpec-3.1-working.docx

Component design guidelines

By designing modular libraries in F#, a developer can reuse components in various other .NET languages. The CLR-based compatibility provides a very practical use case for the developers planning to adapt the F# features gradually in their development environment. These coding conventions and guidelines, presented in the *The F# Component Design Guidelines*, outline the best practices and recommendations for creating class libraries to be used in other .NET programming languages, or by other F# programs. For more information, refer to, http://fsharp.org/specs/component-design-guidelines.

Functional programming guides

Let us take a look at some of the available functional programming guides:

F# for fun and profit

The http://fsharpforfunandprofit.com website introduces the reader to F# and shows how F# can help in the day-to-day development of mainstream commercial business software. These frequently updated resources provide a collection of slides and videos, and an excellent article series on F#. The topics include, but are not limited to, F# versus C#, language conciseness, handling types, design patterns, immutability, concurrency, **DDD (Domain Driven Design)**, and **TDD (Test Driven Development)**.

Data science with F#

Data science is a thriving field which deals with the application and study of machine learning algorithms on real-world data sets. These datasets can be quite large, and creative techniques of statistical analysis have to be used to provide understandable results via visualization. Being a functional language, F# is an excellent resource for data science programming, focused on large scale data-oriented problems. It provides light weight syntax, lazy evaluation, and powerful scripting libraries to help solve big data problems. For more information, refer to http://fsharp.org/guides/data-science/.

This is a guide to libraries that provide the fundamental tools used in data science, a package for high-level exploratory data programming, and interoperability tools for Excel, R, Matlab, Python, and Mathematica.

Math and statistics programming with F#

The functional nature of F# makes it an ideal candidate, and a natural fit, for mathematical problem solving. Functional languages have a long history of assisting with algorithmic proofs, solving numerical problems, and helping with statistical programming. For those interested in the numerical and statistical applications of F#, this is a guide to mathematical and statistical libraries that work well with F#. These libraries are essential for practical numerical transformations, and using F# in a real-world, executable context. For more information, refer to `http://fsharp.org/guides/math-and-statistics/`.

Machine learning with F#

Machine learning is the study of algorithms which can learn and infer from data. This discipline is a combination of various computer science parent fields including, but not limited to, mathematics and statistics, as discussed earlier. F# is proficient in building machine learning applications because of its functional nature, that is, terse mathematical expression style, scalable design, and efficient execution. F# is being used by various advance machine learning groups in both academia and industry, including several groups at Microsoft Research, the birthplace of F#. For more information, refer to `http://fsharp.org/guides/machine-learning/`.

- For more information on F# Mac, Linux, and cross-platform developers guide, refer to `http://fsharp.org/guides/mac-linux-cross-platform`
- **F# Cloud Programming Resources**: `http://fsharp.org/cloud`
- **App and Game Programming with F#**: `http://fsharp.org/apps-and-games`

Books and interactive tutorials

The following are some of the free available online tutorials on F#. These tutorials are excellent resources to learn about different features of the F# programming language in an organized manner. Example coding snippets and interactive lessons (*Try F#*) allow a hobbyist to start experimenting with F# right away, without any lengthy installs. The first functional exposure is always free.

Try F#

If you want to experiment with F# with no commitments, this is the place to go to
`http://www.tryfsharp.org/`. This is a real learning gem published by Microsoft
Research. It helps not only with the F# language itself, but with nice, powerful,
interactive, step-by-step code examples from financial, scientific and numerical,
statistical, data science, and charting applications. It's also a good source for broad,
simple code examples.

The Try F# website provides an interactive environment in the browser to explore. It
is cross-platform (and cross-browser) compatible and contains a variety of tutorials
to cater to different interests. You can refer the following:

- **Getting started in F#**: `http://www.tryfsharp.org/Learn/getting-started`
- **Advanced F# Programming**: `http://www.tryfsharp.org/Learn/advanced-programming`
- **Data Visualization and Charting**: `http://www.tryfsharp.org/Learn/data-visualization`
- **Data Science**: `http://www.tryfsharp.org/Learn/data-science`
- **Scientific and Numerical Computing**: `http://www.tryfsharp.org/Learn/scientific-computing`
- **Financial Computing**: `http://www.tryfsharp.org/Learn/financial-computing`

The F# programming wikibook

This collaborative *wikibook* is a wide-ranging, across-the-board tutorial to F#
programming with code samples. This openly available book comprises of
F# language fundamentals, programming concepts, and information about
multi-paradigm development with F#. For more information, refer to
`http://en.wikibooks.org/wiki/Programming:F_Sharp`.

The information about imperative and object oriented programming in F# is what
distinguishes this guide from rest of the available material. The guide begins with
outlining the fundamentals of working with function and immutable data types,
with examples. It then covers the impure aspects of F# by explaining how to mix
and match object oriented, functional, and imperative styles.

Last but not the least, the wikibook goes advanced, exploring the powerful
abstractions and constructs which F# provides. This includes building multi-
threaded and concurrent applications, async workflows, continuations, reflection,
memoization (caching), and advanced data structures.

The F# workshop

The `http://fsharpworkshop.com/` website contains material from the introduction to *F# Workshop* by Jorge Fioranelli. It is designed to teach you some of the basics of F# and functional programming by combining theory slides (`https://github.com/jorgef/fsharpworkshop/raw/master/FSharpWorkshop_Slides.pptx`) and practice exercises (`https://github.com/jorgef/fsharpworkshop/raw/master/FSharpWorkshop_Exercises.pdf`).

The F# cheat sheet

You can refer to `http://dungpa.github.io/fsharp-cheatsheet/` for more information on F#. It's an F# cheat sheet, a short and sweet introduction to the language syntax.

Video tutorials

The following are some brilliant video tutorials:

- *Pluralsight, Introduction to F#*: Authored by Oliver Sturm, this online course is a primer for the F# programming language. The PluralSight website states *The course will walk you through all of the core details of working with F#, covering not just language fundamentals, but also showing practical scenarios of where it is best used creating .NET application.* For more information on PluralSight, refer to `http://www.pluralsight.com/courses/fsintro`.

- *PluralSight, F# Functional Data Structures*: For more information, refer to `http://www.pluralsight.com/courses/fsharp-functional-data-structures`. Authored by Kit Eason, this course covers the functional data structures using F#. According to the course's website, *This course describes the important data structures - especially collections - available in F#, together with the functions which F# provides for working with them. This course describes the important data structures - especially collections - available in F#, together with the functions which F# provides for working with them.* F# and .NET provide you with a wealth of data structures and collections for storing and manipulating data. This course identifies these structures and the functions which F# provides to work with them, including arrays, lists, and sequences. By the end of the course you'll know how to write idiomatic, maintainable programs which solve complex problems with simple code.

- *PluralSight, A Functional Architecture with F#*: Authored by Mark Seemann, this online course provides an in-depth overview for developing and architecting applications using F#. Refer to, `http://pluralsight.com/training/Courses/TableOfContents/functional-architecture-fsharp`, for further information.

Some miscellaneous video resources are listed as follows:

- F# Talks, tutorials and podcasts can be found at `http://fsharp.org/videos/3`

- MSDN language basics and tutorial videos can be found at `http://msdn.microsoft.com/en-us/vstudio/ff759495.aspx#FLB`

- A list of F# YouTube tutorials can be found at `https://www.youtube.com/playlist?list=PL984822102420AD54`

- F# tutorial with Don Syme (live coding example of analyzing a real-time Twitter feed using F# Interactive) can be found at `http://channel9.msdn.com/Blogs/David+Gristwood/An-F-Tutorial-with-Don-Syme-2-of-4`

Community projects – development tools

The following are some very good development tools:

- **FsEye**: This is a visual object tree inspector for the F# Interactive (`http://www.swensensoftware.com/fseye`)

- **FAKE**: This is an F# build automation system (`http://fsharp.github.io/FAKE`)

- **Paket**: This is a package dependency manager for .NET with support for NuGet packages and GitHub repositories (`https://github.com/fsprojects/Paket`)

- **F# Type Provider starter pack**: This is a NuGet package for writing type providers (`https://github.com/fsprojects/FSharp.TypeProviders.StarterPack`)

- **Community templates for Visual F# Tools**: These are the templates for Visual F# tools (`https://github.com/fsharp/FSharpCommunityTemplates`)

- **F# Project Scaffold**: This is a prototypical F# library (`http://github.com/fsprojects/ProjectScaffold/`)

- **FSharpLint**: This is a lint tool for F# (`https://github.com/duckmatt/FSharpLint`)

- **F# tools for generating documentation**: This is a markdown processor and an F# code formatter (`http://tpetricek.github.com/FSharp.Formatting/`)

Community projects – functional programming

The following are some excellent community projects for functional programming:

- **Streams**: This is a lightweight F#/C# library for efficient functional-style pipelines on streams of data (`http://nessos.github.io/Streams/`)

- **LinqOptimizer**: This is an automatic query optimizer-compiler for Sequential and Parallel LINQ (`http://nessos.github.io/LinqOptimizer/`)

- **ExtCore**: This is a core library extensions for F# (`https://github.com/jack-pappas/ExtCore`)

- **FSharpEnt**: This is a collection of helpers for enterprise development with F# (`https://github.com/colinbull/FSharpEnt`)

- **FSharpx.Collections**: This is a set of functional programming collections for F# (`http://fsprojects.github.io/FSharpx.Collections/`)

- **FSharpx**: These are the extensions and tools for F# Programming (`https://github.com/fsprojects/fsharpx`)

- **F# Snippets**: This is a community-contributed catalog of F# Snippets (`http://fssnip.net/`)

Community projects – data science programming

Some excellent community projects for data science programming are listed as follows:

- **Deedle**: This is a library for data and time series manipulation and for scientific programming and can be found at `http://bluemountaincapital.github.io/Deedle/`

- The Matlab type provider for F# can be found at `http://bayardrock.github.io/Matlab-Type-Provider/`

- The Python type provider for F# (experimental) can be found at `http://fsprojects.github.io/FSharp.Interop.PythonProvider/`

Community projects – the GPU execution

The following are some excellent community projects for GPU execution, a technique for high-performance financial, image processing, and other data-parallel numerical programming.

- **FSCL**: This is a framework for OpenCL programming, scheduling, and execution abstraction on heterogeneous platforms in F# (`http://fscl.github.io/FSCL.Compiler/`)

- **Alea.cuBase**: This is the professional GPGPU programming with F# and CUDA(TM) (`http://blog.quantalea.net/`)

- **Brahma.FSharp**: This is the **General Purpose** (**GP**) GPU programming with F# and is a quotation to OpenCL translator (`https://github.com/gsvgit/Brahma.FSharp`)

General functional programming

The following are some valuable resources on general functional programming:

- *Lambda the Ultimate*: This is a programming languages blog, and can be found at `http://lambda-the-ultimate.org/`

- The *Hole in the middle* pattern by B. Hurt at `http://tinyurl.com/hole-in-the-middle`

- *Syntax Matters*: This includes writing abstract computations in F# by T. Petricek, D. Syme at `http://tomasp.net/academic/papers/computation-zoo/syntax-matters.pdf`

- *Real-World Functional Programming: With Examples in F# and C#*: This includes functional programming with examples in F# and C# by T. Petricek and J. Skeet. Manning, 2009. ISBN 978-1933988924

- *Are Design Patterns Missing Language Features*, retrieved on May 2012, from Portland Pattern Repository (Cunningham and Cunningham) can be found at `http://tinyurl.com/patterns-missing`

- *F# First Class Events: Simplicity and Compositionality in Imperative Reactive Programming* by D. Syme can be found at `http://tinyurl.com/fsharp-events`

And a couple of quick Haskell shout-outs:

- *Programming in Haskell by G. Hutton*, Cambridge University Press, 2007

- *Real World Haskell, B. O'Sullivan, D. Stewart, and J. Goerzen*, O'Reilly 2008

Academic resources

As a popular paradigm for scientists and mathematicians, a majority of functional programming publications emerge from academic circles. The Journal of functional programming, published by Cambridge University Press is an excellent resource to keep up with the advancements in the functional programming paradigm. It is available at `http://journals.cambridge.org/action/displayJournal?jid=JFP`.

As stated on the Journal's website:

> *"Journal of Functional Programming is the only journal devoted solely to the design, implementation, and application of functional programming languages, spanning the range from mathematical theory to industrial practice. Topics covered include functional languages and extensions, implementation techniques, reasoning and proof, program transformation and synthesis, type systems, type theory, language-based security, memory management, parallelism and applications. Special tracks are devoted to tools and applications, commercial uses and education; pearl-type papers are encouraged.*

> *– Cambridge University Press website*

An academic subscription is required to access the journal.

F# foundation maintains a list of academic publications which can be found at `http://fsharp.org/teaching/research.html#functional-programming`.

Pearls of Functional Algorithm Design by Richard Bird is an excellent resource to learn about algorithm design in functional languages. Richard Bird is a professor of computer science at Oxford University and a fellow of Lincoln College, Oxford. This book targets the wannabe functional programmers, academics, and hobbyists alike. Interested in mastering the techniques of reasoning in an equational style? Pick it up!

Another classical text is *Structure and Interpretation of Computer Programs* by Gerald Jay Sussman and Hal Abelson. This book contains discussions of several purely functional data structures such as purely functional streams, along with an implementation of infinite sequences.

Since the dissertation work by Chris Okasaki on pure functional data structures, several new data structures and improvements have been introduced. A simple implementation technique for priority search queues by Ralf Hinze published in ACM SIGPLAN Notices, 2001 provides a simple and elegant technique for implementing priority search queues. Another one of R. Hinze's paper on *Bootstrapping One-sided Flexible Arrays* is published in ICFP '02 Proceedings of the seventh ACM SIGPLAN international conference on functional programming. The approach here is similar to Okasaki's random-access lists, but the one-sided flexible arrays can be tuned to alter the time tradeoff.

Following is a partial list of other notable implementations:

- *Ideal Hash Trees, Fast and Space Efficient Trie Searches* by Phil Bagwell is a good introduction to Trie data structure, and is used as an essential building block in Clojure's STL standard library.

- *Functional Pearl: The Zipper* by Gerard Huet in the Journal of Functional Programming discussed the zipper data structure. This data structure represents *a tree together with a subtree that is the focus of attention, where that focus may move left, right, up or down the tree.*

- *Purely Functional, Real-Time Deques with Catenation* by H. Kaplan and R. Tarjan describes a purely functional implementation as *an algorithmic technique related to the redundant digital representations used to avoid carry propagation in binary counting.*

- *Maxiphobic heaps* by Chris Okasaki, the author of *Purely Functional Data Structures.*

- *Purely Functional Worst Case Constant Time Catenable Sorted Lists*, by Gerth Stølting Brodal, Christos Makris, and Kostas Tsichlas exhibits a data structure which can perform $O(\log n)$ inserts, searches, and deletes and $O(1)$ concatenations.

- *Confluently Persistent Tries for Efficient Version Control* by Erik Demaine, Stefan Langerman, and Eric Price provides information about various functional as well as nonfunctional data structures for tries.

- *The missing method: Deleting from Okasaki's red-black trees* by Matt Might, provides the missing method (delete) implementation on Okasaki's original work.

- *RRB-Trees: Efficient Immutable Vectors* by Phil Bagwell and Tiark Rompf is a discussion on relaxed radix balanced tree provides a heuristic for node shuffling yield. As the paper states, *extension to Hash Array Mapped Tries, supporting immutable vector concatenation, insert-at, and split in $O(\log n)$ time.*

- *Packrat Parsing: Simple, Powerful, Lazy, Linear Time*, an article on functional pearl by Bryan Ford was published in the proceedings of the seventh ACM SIGPLAN international conference on functional programming. The paper discusses Packrat parsing as an original technique for developing parsers in a lazy functional programming language.

- *Breadth-First Numbering: Lessons from a Small Exercise in Algorithm Design* by Chris Okasaki appeared in the proceedings of the fifth ACM SIGPLAN international conference on Functional programming. Also, *Purely Functional Random-Access Lists* by Chris Okasaki which appeared in the proceedings of the seventh international conference on functional programming languages and computer architecture.

- *Alternatives to Two Classic Data Structures* by Chris Okasaki was published in the SIGCSE '05 proceedings of the 36th SIGCSE technical symposium on computer science education. Red-black trees and leftist heaps are classic data structures which are a part of typical data structures and algorithms courses.

- The editorial in *Special issue on Algorithmic aspects of functional programming languages* by Chris Okasaki, published in the **Journal of Functional Programming**, is an educational read for edification on functional programming and data structure. In this editorial, Dr. Okasaki states the case for functional programming and algorithms quite effectively.

  > *"Algorithms can be dramatically affected by the language in which they are implemented. An algorithm that is elegant and efficient in one language may be ugly and inefficient in another. If you have ever attempted to implement an assignment-intensive algorithm in a functional programming language, you are probably more familiar with this phenomenon than you ever wanted to be! But this sword does not cut in only one direction. Functional programming languages are wonderfully suited to expressing certain kinds of algorithms in a clean, modular way, and researchers over the last five to ten years have greatly expanded the range of algorithms for which this is true."*

  Chris Okasaki, Journal of Functional Programming

- *Lightweight Semiformal Time Complexity Analysis for Purely Functional Data Structures* by Nils Anders Danielsson appeared in the proceedings of the 35th annual ACM SIGPLAN-SIGACT symposium on principles of programming languages. This paper's abstract, given next, illustrates a simplistic library for almost fully formal analysis.

- *Full Functional Verification of Linked Data Structures* by Karen Zee, Viktor Kuncak and Martin C. Rinard appeared in proceedings of the 2008 ACM SIGPLAN conference. This paper claims to provide *first verification of full functional correctness* for trees, hash tables, mutable lists, and graphs.

- Auburn, a kit for benchmarking functional data structures was introduced in Springer's *Implementation and Application of Functional Languages*. The abstract outlines that since all purely functional data structures are persistent, Auburn does not only generate the benchmarks for a given data structure but also an explanation of the optimal usage of the data structure. It helps with performance improvement and benchmarking of functional data structures.

- A recent review of *Purely Functional Data Structures* by Kristjan Vedel is also worth reading to get a good grasp of the topic and further enhancements since Okasaki's work. The paper is available at `https://courses.cs.ut.ee/MTAT.03.271/2012_fall/uploads/Main/KristjanVedel.pdf`.

Summary

That's all folks. This was the first step towards the beginning of your functional journey, and you have taken the leap towards learning a new paradigm in thinking and programming. Now that you have been through the entire book (hopefully), it would be quite evident that F# is a powerful functional language, and a great addition to the .NET Framework. As a multi-paradigm language, you can use F# in a pragmatic manner, in both academia and industry, without being restricted to a single paradigm.

In this book, you have explored various data structures, and their uses in algorithms; all of this was kept pretty foundational to provide you the basic knowledge, which can be further improved as you progress. You have learned to use FSI (FSharp Interactive) and learned about the NuGet and F# libraries. With the basic mutable types, you have learned the potential perils of working with side effects, and issues that we may encounter, including exceptions and I/O. You also observed general principles to avoid imperative programming and played with building-blocks of typed functional programming using F#.

F# brings the power of functional programming to the .NET Framework. This book is an introduction to functional programming with F# and an ideal complement to other intermediate to advanced texts. While you may still encounter individuals regarding F# as a niche language, be clear that it's a general purpose Turing complete programming language in which you can build almost any application. It has support for Microsoft .NET runtime, powerful data structures, and expansive built-in libraries and algorithms. This book and the resources provided in this chapter give you a great overview of how to build an application in F#; now it is left to the reader to practice his or her craft and build upon this foundation.

Learning F#, especially if it is your first functional language, will be hard, like learning a foreign language. One way to get over this learning curve is to start coding; so let's get to it. As Linux Torvalds once famously said, "Talk is cheap. Show me the code."

Happy F# Programming!

Index

Symbols

.NET FCL (Framework Class Library) 92
.NET framework 4.5
  URL, for download 23

A

A* (A-star) algorithm 138
Abstract Data Type (ADT) 89, 90
Abstract syntax trees (AST) 118
academic resources
  about 169-171
  URL 169
active pattern 60, 61
ADTs 109
algorithmic complexity
  and Big-O notation 61
App and Game Programming
  with F#, URL 163
arrays 47-51

B

Big-O notation 45, 61, 62
binary search tree 111-114
Brahma.FSharp
  URL 168
Bubble sort 62-66

C

C#
  and F#, syntactical differences 15-17
  and F#, syntactical similarities 15-17
CIL (Common Intermediate Language) 153
CLI (Common Language Infrastructure) 153

Clojure
  about 152
  reference link 152
CloudSharper
  URL 23
collections
  in .NET framework 123
Community templates for Visual F# Tools
  URL 166
Compiler APIs 157
component design guidelines
  about 162
  URL 162
CSV file
  enumerating 78-81

D

data science
  URL 164
  programming 167
  with F#, URL 162, 163
data structures
  about 46, 47
  active pattern 60, 61
  arrays 47-50
  discriminated unions 59, 60
  list comprehensions 53
  lists 51-53
  maps 58
  option types 57
  records 56, 57
  sequences 54, 55
  sets 58
  tuples 56, 57

URL 161
functional programming
  about 1
  general 168
  importance 3, 4
  paradigm, exploring 2, 3
functional programming guides
  about 167
  data science with F# 162
  data science, with F# 163
  F# for fun and profit 162
  machine learning, with F# 163
  math and statistics programming,
    with F# 163
functional queue
  creating 123-125
F# Workshop
  URL 165

G

GPU execution 168
graph 110
Graph#
  URL 143
graphs
  about 134
  data structure 134
  directed graphs 134
  hyper graphs 134
  modeling, F# used 135-137
  undirected graphs 134
  weighted graphs 134

H

Hello World example 6-15
hyper graphs 134

I

ILDASM (IL disassembler)
  about 155
  URL 156
Integrated Development Environments
    (IDEs)
  setting up 22, 23
  URL 22

Intermediate Language (IL) 145, 153
Intermediate System to Intermediate
    System (IS-IS) 137

J

JIT (Just-In-Time) 153

K

key queue operations
  Dequeue (item) 122
  Enqueue (item) 122

L

lazy evaluations
  applying, for sorting 40, 41
LIFO (Last-In-First-Out) 90
LinqOptimizer
  URL 167
list comprehensions 53
lists 51-53

M

machine learning
  with F#, URL 163
MailboxProcessor class, in F# 126-131
maps
  about 58, 145, 146
  example 146
math and statistics programming
  with F#, URL 163
Matlab type provider
  URL 167
memoization
  about 36
  Fibonacci, using 35-37
Merge sort 67-70
Microsoft NGEN (CLR Native Image
    Generator) 153
minimal path sum
  searching 140-143
MSDN
  Assert class, URL 100
  language, URL 166
  URL 51, 99
MSIL (Microsoft Intermediate
    Language) 153

N

n-ary tree 111
nodes 110
NUnit console
    URL 102
n-way trees 111

O

online tutorials
    F# cheat sheet 165
    F# programming wikibook 164
    F# Workshop 165
    Try F# 164
option types 57
OSPF (Open Shortest Path First) 137

P

Paket
    URL 166
PersistentVector 150
PluralSight
    URL 165
print statement (Hello World)
    executing 26-29
priority queue 122
Python type provider
    URL 167

Q

query expression
    developer type 81
    programming language 81
    using 81-84
Queue
    about 122
    data structure, reference 126
    default implementation 122
Quicksort
    about 66, 67
    implementing 41-43
    URL 41

R

records 56, 57
recursion 29-35
recursive functions 8
REPL (Read-Eval-Print Loop) 8
RSA encryption 33

S

Scala 149
Scientific and Numerical Computing, Try F#
    URL 164
Seq.filter function 76
sequences
    about 54, 55, 71-78
    creating, from collections 85, 86
    usage considerations 86
Services APIs 157
set collection 146
sets 58, 145
sets and maps
    revisiting 147-149
shortest-path algorithm 137-140
simple AVL tree 148
simple queue implementation, in F# 122
sorting algorithms
    F# implementation 61
stack
    building 90-95
    testing 96-104
    used, for parenthesis matching 104-107
    with concurrency support 95, 96
Streams
    URL 167

T

TDD (Test Driven Development) 162
Towers of Hanoi
    about 38-40
    rules 38
tree
    Abstract syntax trees 118
    as data structure 110, 111
    binary search tree 111-114
    navigating 114-117

Thank you for buying
Learning F# Functional Data Structures and Algorithms

About Packt Publishing

Packt, pronounced 'packed', published its first book, *Mastering phpMyAdmin for Effective MySQL Management*, in April 2004, and subsequently continued to specialize in publishing highly focused books on specific technologies and solutions.

Our books and publications share the experiences of your fellow IT professionals in adapting and customizing today's systems, applications, and frameworks. Our solution-based books give you the knowledge and power to customize the software and technologies you're using to get the job done. Packt books are more specific and less general than the IT books you have seen in the past. Our unique business model allows us to bring you more focused information, giving you more of what you need to know, and less of what you don't.

Packt is a modern yet unique publishing company that focuses on producing quality, cutting-edge books for communities of developers, administrators, and newbies alike. For more information, please visit our website at www.packtpub.com.

About Packt Open Source

In 2010, Packt launched two new brands, Packt Open Source and Packt Enterprise, in order to continue its focus on specialization. This book is part of the Packt Open Source brand, home to books published on software built around open source licenses, and offering information to anybody from advanced developers to budding web designers. The Open Source brand also runs Packt's Open Source Royalty Scheme, by which Packt gives a royalty to each open source project about whose software a book is sold.

Writing for Packt

We welcome all inquiries from people who are interested in authoring. Book proposals should be sent to author@packtpub.com. If your book idea is still at an early stage and you would like to discuss it first before writing a formal book proposal, then please contact us; one of our commissioning editors will get in touch with you.

We're not just looking for published authors; if you have strong technical skills but no writing experience, our experienced editors can help you develop a writing career, or simply get some additional reward for your expertise.

F# for Quantitative Finance

ISBN: 978-1-78216-462-3   Paperback: 286 pages

An introductory guide to utilizing F# for quantitative finance leveraging the .NET platform

1. Learn functional programming with an easy-to-follow combination of theory and tutorials.

2. Build a complete automated trading system with the help of code snippets.

3. Use F# Interactive to perform exploratory development.

4. Leverage the .NET platform and other existing tools from Microsoft using F#.

Testing with F#

ISBN: 978-1-78439-123-2   Paperback: 286 pages

Deliver high-quality, bug-free applications by testing them with efficient and expressive functional programming

1. Maximize the productivity of your code using the language features of F#.

2. Leverage tools such as FsUnit, FsCheck, Foq, and TickSpec to run tests both inside and outside your development environment.

3. A hands-on guide that covers the complete testing process of F# applications.

Learning JavaScript Data Structures and Algorithms

ISBN: 978-1-78355-487-4   Paperback: 218 pages

Understand and implement classic data structures and algorithms using JavaScript

1. Learn how to use the most used data structures such as array, stack, list, tree, and graphs with real-world examples.

2. Get a grasp on which one is best between searching and sorting algorithms and learn how to implement them.

3. Follow through solutions for notable programming problems with step-by-step explanations.

Windows Phone 7.5 Application Development with F#

ISBN: 978-1-84968-784-3   Paperback: 138 pages

Develop amazing applications for Windows Phone using F#

1. Understand the Windows Phone application development environment and F# as a language.

2. Discover how to work with Windows Phone controls using F#.

3. Learn how to work with gestures, navigation, and data access.

Please check **www.PacktPub.com** for information on our titles

www.ingramcontent.com/pod-product-compliance
Lightning Source LLC
Chambersburg PA
CBHW060600060326
40690CB00017B/3769